CITY LIVES

CITY LIVES

written and photographed by

James Wagenvoord

Holt, Rinehart and Winston   New York

Published simultaneously in Canada by Holt,
Rinehart and Winston of Canada, Limited.

Library of Congress Cataloging in
Publication Data
Wagenvoord, James.
    City lives.

    1. New York (City)—Description. 2. New
York (City)—Social conditions. 3. Wagen-
voord, James.
I. Title.
F128.52.W38 974.7'1'04 75-21492
ISBN Hardcover 0-03-015131-7
ISBN Paperback 0-03-015126-0

First Edition

Designer: Madelaine Caldiero
Printed in the United States of America
10 9 8 7 6 5 4 3 2 1

This book is for
Jennifer, Donn and Harold,
who gave me memories.
And for their children,
Brendon and Dana;
Mitch, Greg and Josh;
and Nicole and Rodman,
who give them life.

Acknowledgments

To name and properly thank all of
the people who helped make this
book would require a companion
volume of equal size. Literally hundreds of city people gave me their
time and their insight and allowed
me repeated glimpses into their
lives. My thanks.

I owe particular credit to Judd
Howard and Paul Curtis. Judd assisted with most of the interviews
and the photography. His excep-
tional talent and feeling for the
realities and dreams of people in a
city became an important element of
this book. Paul Curtis, also an out-
standing young talent, guided me
through parts of the city. His un-
derstanding and sense of the city
was invaluable.

A special thanks also must go to
Patricia Motal and the fine staff at
Motal Photographic Labs, Inc., for
their care and superb effort in printing the photographs used in the
book.

Joe Zinzi, Ed Remson, Bob Tiller,
Jacob Goldstein, Ann Herskowitz,
John Abadio, Leslie Tolbert, Eric
Strickland, Edwin Romberg and
Jack Salazar are just a few of those
who made it possible to begin to ex-
perience the complexities of com-
munities throughout the city. And
Anita, Fumio, Marion, Eleanor,
Dorothy, Peter and Susan, once
again I'm in your debt.

JAMES WAGENVOORD

"The city fosters art and is art.
The city creates the theater
and is the theater."
—Lewis Mumford,
The Culture of Cities

Contents

HERE & THERE

It was an unusual city day, one of those dozen or so a year when mid-afternoon air is crisp and bright sunlight flashes through well-hidden pollutants, leaving horizons clear and sharply etched in the sky. Judd Howard and I walked toward the mouth of the Brooklyn Bridge and saw the crowd in the park facing the well-worn classicism of City Hall. I said, "They're probably shooting a movie," and we turned up onto the pedestrian walk bisecting the bridge and began the stroll up the planked walkway over the East River. It was an ideal day for skyline photographs, just five minutes after three, and it took only three or four minutes to walk far enough to realize that automobile traffic was completely frozen. Sound came not from horns and frustrated drivers but from men in leisure clothes, pounding their palms together in unison, chanting to a self-produced beat,

> CLAP, CLAP, CLAP
> WE DON'T WORK . . .
> THE CI-TY STOPS . . .
> CALL A COP . . .
> CLAP, CLAP, CLAP . . .

Wooden police barricades had been carried into place only moments before on the span's roadways, causing cars to stop a few yards short of the exit ramps, filling the Brooklyn-to-Manhattan lanes. The outbound traffic, barricaded at the entry ramps, was already backing up into the streets feeding into the bridge. Up on the bridge a couple of hundred off-duty officers manned the barricades, flag pins and buttons showing on most of their sport shirts. Except for the incessant chanting, WE DON'T WORK . . . it became strangely quiet . . . THE CITY STOPS . . . Earlier in the day,

as the 8:00 A.M. to 4:00 P.M. shift assembled in precinct station houses throughout the city . . . CALL A COP . . . fifteen hundred policemen had been laid off, furloughed, as one of the first major publicity-staged steps in the city administration's attempt to come to grips with the reality of its lack of financial strength.

As the clapping and chanting continued on the bridge, the head of the Policemen's Union mounted a portable speaker's stand in front of City Hall. Massaged by television news cameras, he began his electronically amplified statement designed to filter through his immediate spectators and, through lenses and microphones, to the city's homes and apartments. Fault and blame for a mayor and some unnamed state senators. Courage and plaudits for the city's finest, the brave, staunch men in blue. Shadows and fear for people told that they lived in an "unprotected" city. There was no mention that 29,300 policemen were still policemen, earning solid middle- and upper-middle-class salaries. Now, on the walkway, well onto the bridge, away from the speaker's stand, it seemed reasonable to me to scale the protective fence, drop the short distance to the roadway, and take some pictures. The best pictures would be from down there, aiming directly into the protesters. But after gaining the roadway I had only time to focus before I saw a lens full of close-up faces and, with Judd, became the target of disjointed, frantic shouts. "No pictures. We don't want no pictures." It didn't make sense—after all, this action was just part of a media-oriented protest. Weren't they all?

"You a Communist?"

"Gimme that camera!"

"No pictures or we throw your ass off this bridge."

A hand reached out for the camera. I reflexively held the camera to my chest and discovered that I was scared, really scared. For the first time in my adult years in the city I knew I was involved in a moment completely beyond my control. "See down there?" An angry young man gestured through a space in the bridge frame down to the street. "Your camera's going down . . . and then you're going after it."

I found enough air in my lungs to blurt out, "You're not going to do that."

"Why not?"

"Because you're a policeman." My reasoning rang as hollow then as it reads now.

"Not anymore, pal," he shouted. "We're ex-cops. We've been laid off." He grabbed roughly for my camera and at that moment another "ex-cop" crashed through the men surrounding us. He quickly got us out of the crowd, across the roadway, and onto the walk. As we headed back down the bridge, momentary fear turned to anger—safe, nonthreatening anger, for neither of us was about to direct any emotion at the protesters. On our left half a dozen "ex-cops" loudly harassed a young couple who, straddling a motorcycle, had inadvertently gained access to the bridge. Hands grabbed at the exposed chrome parts of the Honda's motor. The girl on the second cushion held tightly to the driver; his frozen stare aimed straight ahead. To their rear, a car, a new Pontiac which had followed

the motorcycle onto the ramp, was also surrounded. The driver's door was yanked open and the shouts of young men, ringing with the thrill of an adult tantrum, brought the same glazed look of terror to the eyes of the middle-aged driver in business dress.

We left the bridge, an aftertaste of emotional nausea in our throats over the feeling of being controlled absolutely by individuals acting as a mob. In front of City Hall the union leader was reaching the final phrases of his scripted statement. It was still midafternoon, the air was still crisp and had not lost its brilliance, the downtown skyline was spectacular. In two and a half hours the local television newscasts would be playing brief excerpts of the speech. Traffic was about to resume rolling, and uniformed policemen were already moving into position to wave cars onto the arterial streets. Another demonstration was on its way to becoming a minor incident.

CLAP, CLAP, CLAP . . .

THE CITY STOPS . . .

But not quite, not yet.

I began walking through a city, looking for neighborhoods, as winter slush was beginning to turn to spring mud. That was in the "old days," several weeks before hand-distributed flyers and press-disseminated politico-publicity reports proclaimed that I was living in "Fear City." City bonds as an investment were still considered, at least in the public press, as sure things, inviolate. There hadn't been a slowdown in garbage collection for nearly a year, I could still ride a bus or subway somewhere and return and have change for a dollar, and six of the eight buildings I had lived in during my years in the city were still standing. Truly the old days.

Now, less than a year later, Federal Reserve municipal guarantees, emergency bond issues, strikes and sick-outs over cost-of-living clauses in public employment union contracts are subjects glibly spoken of and dismissed. And the incredible pace of "crisis" begetting "crisis" continues to accelerate. Within this emotional urban wind tunnel neighborhoods were at first elusive, at least the geopolitical type of neighborhood that is spoken of in official pronouncements. For instance, sitting in the Office of Neighborhood Services, a mayoral department which by its name would seem to be a valid starting point, I found it tempting to give up the search. The "neighborhood" of Flatbush, one of the two-dimensional areas outlined in red on a large wall map, has a population in excess of one hundred fifty thousand—a few thousand less than Hartford, Connecticut. Crown Heights, a partial political label for one of the smallest areas on the map, contains over fifty thousand individuals—large enough to be one of the top ten cities in Iowa. There is, of course, nothing of significance in such size comparisons. The contrasts, the automatic writing of disposable information lists, i.e., the softest, the hardest, the meanest, the most gentle, etc., have nothing to do with the reality of living in a city. Specifically it has nothing to do with living in direct relationship to other people within a "neighborhood." In political offices, from spectator platforms atop skyscrapers, in the pages of newspapers, and on television screens, everything is "there." Come out into the streets and walk along the sidewalks and you begin to feel the "here" of a city. And if you move away from the points where public transportation intersects you begin to find the twenty-four-hour-a-day, everyday, living city.

The places that mean home to the people who give a city its blood and breath can be honestly defined only by the individuals who live there. Ask yourself what makes "here" in your own life. At what point, what mental line, when you leave your home, do you stop feeling completely familiar, completely at home? At what point in any direction does the word "here" become "there"? "Here" is the neighborhood.

Rudyard Kipling wrote, "There are but two kinds of people in this world. One who stays at home—the other who is always away from home." The truth of his statement can be nowhere more easily witnessed than in the world's cities. In New York, for the most part, those who write its public lyrics, count its money, run its factories, design its buildings, and determine its urban themes are away from home—having come to the city to fulfill a pop-primeval urge for power and recognition (usually to make a point back home). And consistently obscured in the rhetoric and imagery are the millions to whom the city is indeed home, who were born into its brass and noise and dust and enforced anonymity, have aunts, uncles, cousins, grandparents, friends of the family, and who, in many instances, represent a second or third generation in the same public or parochial school. I'm writing now of whites, for although the Puerto Ricans and blacks have, in many cases, been here for up to three and four generations, they are viewed by home-city whites as interlopers who still have the sense of a place to which they can return, or still possess an awareness of a place to which they vow they will never return.

9

It's easy these days to forget that, like it or not from your own personal perspective, every person who lives in a city *lives* in a city. For example, this excerpt from an article about New York's financial quandary in the magazine *New Times:*

When a stranger speaks to you here, you brace yourself. Odds are that you are about to be panhandled, propositioned, or punched.

Out there, in the land of Kiwanis and double-knit suits and white patent leather shoes, the good people who are the backbone of this country can content themselves. Their taxes may be going up, their teachers getting restless, their kids turning on, but at least it isn't New York. New York is a disease. And probably a necessary one. If there weren't a New York it would have to be somewhere else. Someone has to suffer, if only so everyone else can feel better by comparison.

None of this bothers New Yorkers. It's not that they don't like all the nice things that go on in places like Cincinnati and Butte and Anaheim, or that they enjoy being hassled and hustled, tensing whenever they see a black teenager in tennis shoes (they are called "Perpetrator boots" hereabouts) ambling toward them.

This is similar to most of the writing and reporting that repeats itself day after day. But it's flawed. Seriously flawed. That "black teen-ager in tennis shoes" is a New Yorker. He calls those shoes Adidas or Pumas or just plain sneaks, and the odds are tremendously good that he will continue ambling right past the media "New Yorker" and move on to where he is headed. Those mythological antagonists who in commentators' terms are invariably cocked to go off with a panhandle or proposition or punch are also of the city. They may not be crisp and slick and commercial, and they are candidates for nonperson slotting by the press, but they live in the city. And perhaps if answered they might not panhandlepropositionpunch but merely ask directions or offer the same. And those folks in the heartland, the club joiners, the double-knit and white-patent-leather-shoe wearers, my God, you might not bump into them in a media man's bar or in the Hamptons, but you will bump into them in the city. They live here too.

The photographs in this book were made as two-dimensional notes. Thinking of the camera within such a framework during an era marked by an art industry boosting photography as fine art causes some self-consciousness. Right in the heart of the city, only a few blocks from that fabled corner in Times Square, there is a camera repair company called Professional Camera Repair. I go there every few months to have my cameras cleaned, checked, and, all too often, repaired. Photography may or may not be a broad-based fine art medium—that's an argument that will continue for years—but there is also another form, a largely unnoticed, adjunct form, of photography, and it is growing. It is this area, the adjunct, that has had the strongest influence on the pictures in this book. I became aware of it a year ago, while leaning on the counter at Professional Camera. On my side of the counter there were seven people, all bearing Leicas or Nikons. Five of the customers were from federal or local undercover law enforcement agencies. As I worked on this book, it became more and more apparent to me that, at least as regards the photography, I met the competition at Professional Camera.

The law-defending, undercover photographers have been both a plus and a minus. The man who gave me my start with cameras once explained to me that, within my interests, the camera could serve as a passport. This has proven to be true. On the streets it gives a reasonable function, a reason to strike up conversations, if no more than asking permission to take a photograph. And it provides a reason to return, to show the photograph. But people who spend part of their lives on sidewalks and streets in cities— particularly in areas officially considered "in transition" (this means black or Puerto Rican, or less then middle-class-dominated)—are aware of what's going on. The appearance of a male, over twenty- five, white, with a camera, by

himself, on a weekday brings forth frequent identification as an undercover man. This is not just a middle-aged fantasy, for throughout the year the question asked of me most often was simply, "Are you a cop?" This has been the plus. Some confrontations that were forced turned into friendships. It's also the minus, for it made the familiarization process with a number of people take more time until they could be comfortable with me or simply trust me—trust me as a person, as a writer, and as a photographer. It's too easy to cheat, particularly with

a camera, to come in close, catch
a moment or an attitude that
really isn't there. That's a television
trick which seems to have been per-
fected during the years of news-
accommodating protests. You can
fill a lens with ten people and with
professional cropping give a feeling
that there are hundreds more just
beyond the frame. More often than
not it's just the ten who are stating
their desires—otherwise the camera
would pull back and show more.
Think about it. In real life, not in
photographic note-taking, there
continues to be a relationship with
space and a continuing visual field
that gives an honest proportion. I
don't mean that everything has to be
viewed from a distance. Only that if
you come in close, in tight, emotionally or optically, you should be *be*
close—not just enjoy the appearance
of being close.

IMAGES

The Building

It is known as "The Building" to the people who live in it. And if there really is a melting pot, it probably is this. The city certainly isn't one, and the older districts, which stretch throughout the maze that represents the map-makers' view of life, still retain a singular ethnic or racial or cultural character. But in The Building, one of the many "luxury" rental apartment houses in the "safer parts" of the city, race and religion slip away as cheek-by-jowl differences. The only qualifier is the ability to withstand or slip through a credit check—to demonstrate that an individual or a family has the ability to pay one-and-a-half times the national monthly minimum wage in rent alone. And pay consistently for at least twenty-four months.

Instead of a series of stoops or a block-long sidewalk there is "the club," a slickly styled, tower-top amalgam of green Astroturfed sundecks, a swimming pool surrounded by red, white, and blue lounge chairs, a dining room, and separate but very equal exercise and sauna facilities for men and women. The rooftop makes a difference. It makes some of the people feel like neighbors. Not all of the people, for, as in every block, or street, or neighborhood in the country, there are some who prefer to live lives apart from others. But on the rooftop, just as on the stoops, people meet other people. Up at the club, pregnancies are witnessed, drinks are downed, opinions on the value of present children are traded, swimmers mentally count out forty-foot lengths in the mid-eighty-degree water, courtships and occasional one-night or one-afternoon stands are overseen, affairs are rumored, and the basic antipathy between young, middle-

"I met a woman on my floor one morning. I was passing her in the hall and I said, 'What have you been doing lately?' And she said, 'I was on Captain Kangaroo this morning,' which I loved. My God, a neighbor who really knows Mr. Greenjeans!"

—A TENANT

19

aged, and old is analyzed, over-analyzed, and debated. All the while roots, even if they are no deeper than the fragile tendrils shot into the earth by strawberries, grab hold for a few city seasons.

This melting pot, however, is more a crêpe pan. There may be a terrific neighbor next door who is black, but there are still Negroes, or worse, even niggers, out there in the city. The wife of an Asian junior diplomat may be stuffing two quarters and her wash into the machines in the laundry room adjacent to the elevators, but those former war-zone Asians being relocated throughout the country remain a quantum leap from being sought as fellow citizens. That young WASP couple—they may be interesting to talk with and occasionally to laugh with, but outside there is still a world that hesitates to take its Jews for granted. Yet a reminder that none of this matters too greatly comes on the first of each month. Testimony to economic equality is given by over six hundred lease-holders.

Late in weekday afternoons and early in the evenings, when people come home, come back to The Building, an understated pride can be witnessed. They may be tired from a day in the office making deals, or shopping or working with clients or handling patients, but a look of confidence is there, more often than not, as the revolving door makes its deposit into the over-sized, thickly carpeted lobby. There are nods and familiar first-name greetings to cocoa-uniformed door attendants and to the "Concierge" behind his walnut desk. And looks of calm recognition if one of the star tenants happens to be momentarily sharing the lobby. The all-pro basketball

mother. I put her down in the grass and she screamed. At first I couldn't understand why she was crying. She was just terrified of the grass, afraid, probably because I've always had her in the stroller and her playground has been the city. I didn't know whether it was the fresh air, or what. I mean, it was just too much for her . . . and for me, to think that the baby was nine or ten months old and had never felt grass. She wouldn't sleep either because the wind in the leaves made too much noise. I felt guilty about it for a week, but I'm certain the city has more advantages. Here I can take her past a cement mixer truck and she won't stir. It lulls her to sleep. Even the fire engines at night, which still wake me, don't affect her. I think the only thing she misses are steps. She doesn't quite yet have the idea of steps . . . that they go someplace, which I think most children have. When she climbed up my parents' steps and got to the second floor, she had no idea where she was. She didn't want to crawl around and explore. She misses something like that, but I don't know how relevant it is. I really don't. In the summer if I want to sunbathe, or any time during the year, if I feel like swimming or relaxing, I just take her up to the roof. And because of the roof and the pool, with the interaction of people, she's not afraid of anybody. She's not timid because she sees so many people up there. That, I think, is important. I don't think it's terribly relevant that the baby knows what grass is because, when she's fifteen years old, I can always say, 'This is green and it is grass,' and if she can't accept it, that's her problem."

player is spoken to only if he's enjoying a hot streak; the evangelist, who everybody knows has the shiniest Rolls-Royce in the garage and gives the biggest tips in the building to the staff at Christmas, is never spoken to; the pop musician, or the actor, in town from the other coast for a few weeks, is offered eye contact.

As is the case everywhere, confidence is countered by doubts and what the over-the-counter drug sellers call "those day-to-day uncertainties." A young mother with the look and movements of a cosmetics model has to consider the question of whether the city is the place to bring up her child.

"Just a couple of months ago we took our daughter down to visit my

Problems. Family problems. Neighbor problems. Living problems. They are found in villages and in cities. Living closely together, with lives separated by six-inch walls and ten-inch ceilings, regardless of consumer levels, gives birth to obsessive "interaction."

"All right, maybe it wasn't the kind of thing where one had to draw the line. But losing the *Times*, having it stolen morning after morning for three weeks while paying nearly a one-hundred-percent premium to be able to open the door and have the paper right there—it's pretty irritating. Not being able just to wake up, sit in my bathrobe, drink coffee, and find out what I should be offended by was bad enough, but what really got to me was that, three days out of four, the thief returned the paper sometime after noon. A used paper. With coffee and egg stains.

"All right, it wasn't a big problem compared to everything else that's going on in the world, but it kept growing. Once I thought I had the thief. Like Kissinger at the height of his power, I passed a signal that I was aware of just what the hell was going on. It was Tuesday morning of the third week. I was up early enough to hear the delivery man drop the paper outside the door. So I picked it up, pulled out the inside pages of both the first and second sections, put the coffee-stained pages from the day before back inside, and placed the whole thing back out in the hall. The thief struck. And I read a paper that started with page three and lacked op-ed and the television listings. Bad enough, but again the damn thing, with even more stains, came back during the day. It was obvious that this was going to go on as long as I paid to have the paper delivered. I had had it. I decided I was going to catch the thief, end the idiocy once and for all, and be able to read a newspaper at my leisure. I set it up with the man at the newstand and the next morning he called me at a quarter to seven to let me know that the paper was on the way up. As traps go mine was pretty primitive. I taped a piece of thread to the paper, ran it under the door, and held it from the inside. Fishing for the diabolical newspaper thief. So there I

was at seven o'clock in the morning, in a luxury apartment in the world's most exciting city, sitting on the floor in my shorts and bathrobe, staring at a door and holding a thread in my hand. After half an hour I was uncomfortable and feeling pretty stupid. Nothing had happened except I knew that I was sitting on the floor with a thread in my hand and my newspaper, with all that great insight, was just a few inches away on the other side of a thin door. I didn't give up. Instead, I looped the thread over the doorknob and joined my wife on the sofa. We sat there sipping coffee, staring at the door. Finally I said, 'The hell with it, I'm going to get the paper. I just want to read the paper.' And at that moment the string flashed over the doorknob and vanished under the door. It was sensational. I was about to have the thief. I ran out into the hall forgetting that I hadn't had a belt on my robe for nearly two years.

"A black-haired woman in a floor-length brown robe was moving away from me toward the service stairway. I shouted back to my wife through the open door, 'Call the desk, dammit, call the desk!' and I saw the woman pass the service door and go straight down the hall.

"Now, while I was trailing my thief my wife picked up the house phone, dialed the lobby desk, and realized that she had nothing to say to the doorman except that her husband was wandering around the hall in his underwear and no belt on his bathrobe. She hung up. The woman turned into an apartment near the end of the hall and slammed the door shut. I heard the safety lock click and began ringing the bell with one hand and pounding on the door with the other. After a few sec-

onds the door opened. Slowly. I couldn't believe it. The only man I knew on the floor, a Japanese, was standing in the foyer. I could hear sobs, his American wife's sobs, coming from the bedroom. And on a small table just to the right of the door I saw the newspaper. All of my fantasized invective left me. Like a dummy I said, 'Excuse me, I think your wife took my paper.'

"He picked it up from the table and said, 'Oh, is this yours?' Then he handed it to me.

"The disgusting thing was that the damned thread was still hanging from it and I had to reel it in before he could close the door. My wife was laughing when I got back to the apartment. She had recognized the woman, but the newstand guy was shocked when I told him who the thief was. All he could say was, 'Who would believe it? The Japanese are such honorable people.' Then he called their apartment and asked them if they wanted to subscribe to the *Times*. Delivered right to their door. They said no.

"That afternoon is the only time I ever ran into the man outside of the building. We were both in the same midtown bank. He came up to me and instead of apologizing, he said, 'I told my wife she should get her own paper. I never bothered with it. I get one at the office.' And I was still feeling embarrassed about reeling in my thread.

"I didn't see the woman again for about six weeks. I came off the elevator and saw her down the hall, sliding a handbill under a door. She put it under the door and then scooped up the newspaper that was lying on the floor. She saw me, dropped the paper, and went on down the hall with her handbills. The handbill was about a tenants'

association meeting and she, God knows how, was suddenly the representative for my floor. I've never gone to a tenants' association meeting. My representative is a goddamn felon."

Were there people in Valhalla who spent their leisure hours trying to organize block and tenant groups? That's a question that may someday be addressed in a degree thesis at the end of a curriculum in city planning. The Building got its organization within a year after its hallway carpets were in place. The existence of a tenant association was greeted by a few outspoken advocates and a few outspoken critics. And it gave some, mainly the "singles" looking for a way to meet others, something to try out. For the most part, however, it was swallowed up by The Building. But a bulletin board was

posted in the main service hallway, and a public telephone was screwed to the wall in an out-of-view corner of the lobby—at the request of the committee.

"It was funny, the tenants' meeting the other night. The reason I went was not because of any desire to discuss any problems in the building but because I did think it was going to be some kind of a social thing, and that there would be some women there. I'm just misguided enough to think that I'm actually going to meet people at one of those things. As I walked through the door I was just too embarrassed to turn around and walk out. But I knew immediately that it was a waste of time. There wasn't much of a crowd, maybe thirty or forty people, and it was made up mainly of older couples and a few hyperintense-looking younger couples.

"I've been in the real world for three years now. And before I came into the business I taught for three years. I always took it for granted when I was teaching that other instructors and professors would be impractical. A friend who taught music used always to say, 'My God, life is just too much for me.' I finally said to him, 'You have no decisions whatsoever. For you a tough decision for the year is when to get your tires rotated. You really have no responsibility, no decisions, nothing to agonize over in teaching the same course time after time.' When I left teaching I really believed that businessmen, particularly in this city, were tough, rational, and sensible . . . that there was a normal person who could handle things. Well, whatever myths I held along those lines were wiped out at the tenants' meeting. I couldn't believe it. I thought I was back as an undergraduate, at a house meeting . . . a bad house meeting, the ones that would go on for four hours, where people felt that the entire agenda should be anecdotal. I heard dog stories, countless dog stories—'Well, you know, ten dogs got on the elevator and I said to the woman, "Would you please wait and let me take this elevator first," and she said, "These dogs have a right to be on this elevator," and isn't that ridiculous?' And then someone said, 'Well, why don't the dogs use the service elevator?' and someone else pointed out that if you had a pet in the building, and they do allow pets, and you had to wait for the laundry rooms service elevators every time, you'd have to wait forty-five minutes. Anyway, it reminded me, I was walking along Madison Avenue with my aunt one day and I told her about a no-end discussion my mother and another aunt had had. And she proceeded to get involved in the same discussion with me as though that were the point. It was frustrating. The meeting was making me begin to think in anecdotes. It was really hard for me to believe the people there were adults who had anything else to do with their time. The typical procedures were going on, like, 'I think that the laundry rooms are disgusting,' and so forth, and so on, and the chairman would say, 'Fine, you're now on the cleanliness committee,' or whatever the committee was. They discussed the laundry rooms and then there was an extended discussion on Christmas tipping. But nothing was ever decided. Some people would say, 'Yeah, that's a good idea,' and some said, 'No, that's not a good idea.' And the roaches, there was a discussion about the 'roach problem' with the same kind of intensity as politicians talk about the 'drug problem' or the 'problems of the aged.' Someone said, 'Well, someone should find out exactly what kind of spray the exterminators are using.' Now I think that if somebody walked into my apartment and started spraying poison all over the place I would at least take a look at the can, or ask about it. You shouldn't have to form a committee to go to the building management to find out what is being used. . . . Anyway, it was less the subject matter, which was absurd, than the lack of any kind of procedure, any type of structure, which sent me out into the night. And it was interesting to me that when I was leaving, a woman I did know also started to walk out. A couple of people sort of hissed at us as though we were doing something wrong, acting like fascists, in leaving!"

The most striking element of life in The Building is not its own physical presence. It is what can be seen by looking out from within. The views are monumental. The visual mythology of the city films of the forties and fifties becomes a glass-protected backdrop for actual lives. Still, the reality of marking out an individual place remains greater than the possibilities for reflection. Particularly for a young businessman seeking to become part of, and to control, his immediate environment—in search of a neighborhood while standing in the neighborhood.

"I've bought a lot of ice cream at the ice cream parlor across the street, and it just galls the shit out of me that whoever's behind the cash register, or behind the counter, or the waitresses . . . I've been in

there fifty times and they don't know me. Dammit, it's irritating, because I want to have these places. I want to have neighborhood places. I don't care if the food's great or not. . . . I'd just like to have somebody that knows you live here. Otherwise, this is just a box and I put rugs and furniture in it.

"And what is the definition of a neighborhood? Theoretically you have neighbors who are not strangers. Neighbors—it means more than just physical proximity. Damn, it really is frustrating. I mean, there are other things in life besides your work. For instance, one of my great pleasures is when people come to visit me. This is my town. 'What do you want tickets to? What do you want to see, what kind of food do you enjoy? We have everything here. Lebanese? Kuwaiti?' And I would love to be able to take people to 'my place' in the neighborhood. Just to say, 'Hey, come on. We can get us some drinks. We can do this,'—you know, to show that not only do I know this city, but that, to some extent, the city recognizes, knows, that I live here.''

Urban Geography

Gray storm clouds scud across the sky exhaling soft bass moans. The late-afternoon mugginess has broken and the first drops of rain chase the people who have been clustered on the sidewalks back into the electric-fan-roiled heat of their buildings. A metallic glow from television screens comes up in several of the front windows. Behind the windows attention is drawn away from the street talk of who's in trouble, who's pregnant, who got drunk or stoned, who's out of a job, who just found one. Instead the focus is given over to making or waiting for dinner and reruns of aging television series. The local news will be on in a few minutes.

It is a neighborhood that has no name—an accident in urban geography. Just a few blocks to the south are the still soot-free walls of the new Ruppert Village, a tight grouping of buildings ranging in height from sixteen to forty-three floors. Before the year is over, sixty-five hundred people will live in this new, institutionally landscaped and terraced, federally funded, centrally air-conditioned village. To the east less than two hundred yards away, stand the weathered and still substantial Stanley Isaacs Houses, one of the nation's first experiments in city-financed, administered, selected-tenant, and rent-supplemented living. West, a block up the steep hill, are the town houses, private, old-line and fast-rich homes, and a scattering of three-room "quaint" apartments with wood-burning fireplaces and views of private gardens—way stations for young, on-their-way-up professionals. Directly north—uptown—lies the first cousin, the Barrio with its distinct connotations

"I was married a long time but my husband left me over twenty years ago. We never got along, he beat me all the time . . . a German, he never took me anywhere, never gave me anything . . . except holes in my shoes."

—AN OLD WOMAN ON THE STOOP

and its own collective sense of reality. But at this curious, now rain-washed, extended intersection, a shard of a city is held together by its lack of connection with anything other than its own location.

On the Avenue, behind a narrow, boarded-over window and a bright green door, the patrons of the Guyamo Social Club crowd around a coin-operated, two-thirds-size pool table. Ernest and Carl are playing out their delicate eight-ball-call-the-pocket shots. And the onlookers, enveloped by the music of James Brown, sipping beers paid for at the small bar in the back of the room, talk easily about who and what and to and from. There are no women in this room. Only the big guys, aged between sixteen and thirty. In the crowd are two young men who, within three months, will know whether or not they are liable to spend their next years in prison. They joke comfortably with a friend over the way people live "upstate." Just "upstate."

"I lived there for three summers, you know. Those workers they ship in up there—shit, man, they don't know nothing."

"Yeah, ya mean the migraines. The migraine workers."

"Yeah, you know, migraines. Those dumb sons-a-bitches, they work in the fields all day long and when they're not working, ya know, they live in shacks so far back in the woods that they hafta pipe in their sunlight."

The cue ball drifts, hesitates, and then plonks into a side pocket. Carl has scratched. Ernest beams and speaks rapidly to himself and to the remaining balls on the table.

Down the Avenue and around the corner, a few yards into the side street, a gray stoop, worn by lost seasons, retains the dampness of the light rain. Flanking lines of dented aluminum garbage cans testify to the fact that this particular arrangement of concrete slabs is a passageway and a piece of furniture. For thirty-four and a half years this has been Rosie's place, Rosie's stoop. Except in impossible weather and for rare bed-dictating illnesses, late each day throughout modern American history, Rosie has walked up the block from her tiny apartment and arranged herself on the top step for the twilight and the evening. She listens and she watches. And she talks.

"One crook, he's one of the biggest crooks around here, he sells a lot of meat. He just come out of the hospital, his liver's gone, but he won't stay in. Even the cops know about him. I know. He sells meat. It's stolen. He goes around to stores and to people he knows in this building. Has it all wrapped up in cellophane. He told me, he said, 'I didn't kill nobody!' He said, 'I take it from the rich, I sell it to the poor,' but I said to him, 'Thou shalt not steal, you know.' I ate from it already 'cuz some people invited me. I tell ya, I thought I was gonna choke on it. I didn't, but every time I was thinking about it I said, 'Oh God, don't punish me' . . . because I don't believe in it. . . . Like one time I was so warm and I wanted to buy a fan from a colored crook. And he said to me, 'Rose, you gotta give me the whole seventeen dollars right away,' and I didn't have the money. But I didn't give a damn. I was too hot and it was late at night. So I took it and the next morning I gave it back to him."

"A friend of mine was the super down the block . . . I used to help him out but he's too old. I still put the cans back in front of that building. He lives in my building now. His sister, she don't want him to work no more and I heard he goes to heart clinic . . . he's got water and his legs are sore, sore for years. He used to visit an old lady next door here. She had an accident and she was getting better, but then she died. A seventeen-year-old Puerto Rican fella backed up quick and she went to pick up her little doggy and the dog ran away and her leg was squashed. She lost the leg and she got pneumonia in the hospital and she dies, poor old woman. Then her daughter, her youngest daughter, both her kidneys were gone and she was living in an electric machine and a sister of hers wanted to give her a kidney. But that sister's husband wouldn't allow it. And she died. Then her husband married her best friend because some of the children were small . . ."

"My super put a dispossess on me once because he's a louse . . . he's no good, that's why. I never got a concession when I came here. Years ago when I came, when you took rooms, they gave you two weeks or a month free, and I never got nothing. After a coupla years my husband was outa work and for two weeks we couldn't pay up. And then fifteen or seventeen years later, the super, he looks in his rent book and puts a note under the door to pay the old two weeks, he had a nerve. But I couldn't pay 'cuz my husband had left me and the Welfare wouldn't pick it up. I still haven't paid him those two weeks. He's a mean bastard . . . he comes this way sometimes, he's a rotten, skinny, skeleton bastard. I can't stand him.

"There used to be a lot of Hungarians here. I'm Hungarian. The man that just went by, he is too. He was working in an apartment building. It was hard for him to get a job, he couldn't talk English. And he always has to look for a Hungarian super, you know, where he can talk with him, and then they put him on back elevator. The front elevator, you know, all the tenants, they ain't gonna be Hungarian, right? If they're born here they wanta talk English, right?"

"That Edgar Hoover, the FBI who died back there, a coupla years. I seen in the paper he left all that money to his friend. Oooow, Hoover was tough-looking, but he was some man, he knew his business. He wanted to retire years ago but they wouldn't let him. He knew his stuff. They're born with it, right? It's like any field, right? And he left his friend his estate and everything and then his friend, he died too. Now where's it gonna go? I hope the man had somebody. Hoover was never married and I don't think the other man was either. That's okay—they're better off, marriage don't last anyway, it's no good. It was no good with my husband. I'm in rags now, I was in rags then. . . . Well, he couldn't afford it but he always managed to get him and my son things. But me? I was left out all the time. Once when I asked my younger sister for a coupla sheets she said she ain't got any, and my husband said, 'Oh, I found sheets,' and he put one on his bed and one on my son's bed. And I said to him, you know, I . . . I let them keep it."

32

On the corner, as the street lamps glow, overlapping the dusk, three young men lounge against the steel-web-protected shop fronts. They've known this particular corner for only two, at the most three, years. They pass a brown-bagged bottle of vodka back and forth and between drinks survey the light traffic. The most physical of the three, a teen-ager with the carriage of a bandy rooster and middle-aged eyes, watches a taxicab roll slowly down the avenue.

"The police oughta get some new cabs for their plainclothes. They've had that taxi for two years now. They roll by every day, all day. We get tired of them and I know when they're coming past. They got the same old beat all the time. And now you got walking cops, you got lady cops. They shouldn't have lady cops out here because a lot of them gonna get hurt. Me, myself, I ain't gonna let no lady take me to jail. She gotta have her gun out and be ready to shoot 'cause if she got it in the hol-ster I'm gonna fight her. I ain't gonna let her take me. A lot of peo-ple ain't gonna let no lady take them to jail. Can you imagine someone sit-ting up there in jail and they say, 'Who arrested you?' 'Oh, Miss Brooks.' 'MISS BROOKS? What the hell she doin' arrestin' you?' You'd be the laughin' stock of the prison. Don't nobody want no lady to take them to jail. They should put them down there where them prostitutes are. Don't put them ladies uptown. Those dudes ain't gonna let ladies take 'em to jail."

"I do all types of things. I sell hot jewelry sometimes. If I know a cou-ple of people and they're comin' out with six, seven thousand dollars'

worth of jewelry, I'll sell it for so much—'cause I know a fence I can sell anything to. If somebody's got some fur coats I'll sell 'em for him. But he's gotta give me something. If he's got a six-thousand-dollar fur coat and will give me five or six hundred dollars, I'll sell it. I sell anything anybody wants me to sell just as long as I get something. Even guns. A gun's about the easiest thing to come by out here. Some-body want a gun all they gotta do is ask. Go around and say 'You know where I can buy a gun?' You may not get the one you wanted but you'll find something. Somebody out here got one that they don't need. Or they did something with it and want to sell it real quick, for around two hundred dollars. In a store a good gun'll cost a hundred or a hundred and fifty dollars. But a person with a record can't buy a gun. Even if he was arrested fifty years ago he still can't buy a gun. I bought my gun on the street about three months ago and if I was to sell it right now I could get more than two hundred dollars. I don't carry it. If I get caught with a gun I'll never get out. If the gun was used to kill somebody they accuse you of it. If I was to sell a gun and I killed somebody yesterday and I sell it to you today and you get caught with it you got to take that murder rap. And I don't want to take a murder rap. That's a long time. Just the other day I sold a couple of antique knives, old-time knives, Samurai swords. A guy had them. I told him that I would sell them for seventy-five dollars. But I sold them for more than I told him I was gonna sell them for. . . . He wanted six hun-dred for everything. I sold them for seven hundred. I made a hundred and seventy-five dollars off him. I sell to the people, people on the street. I sell to people I know. You can sell anything right here in the city. Anything, I don't care what it is. Right now if I rob somebody's apartment and get a color TV I won't have it for ten minutes. Somebody'll buy it. Anything can be sold, I don't care what it is. Sometimes people give me a phone call and say 'I got some hot shit, man.' I even sold hot cars to people. All they want is the engine, they don't want the body. Give me two hundred dollars for the whole car. They get caught that's their problem. Once I give it to them I don't care what happens. Right here in the neighborhood there are a lot of fences. There used to be a bar down the street—it was the biggest fence place in the neighborhood until the police closed it down. You could go in there, walk in with anything, walk out you ain't got it no more. You figure a fence'll pay you half the price for anything. He get back downtown he's gonna get more than he paid. He might just get ten dollars more but he's gonna make a profit. I used to want to run numbers but I couldn't get up at six in the morning and be out there waitin' for those people to go to work. I thought it was an afternoon job. But it's mornings. I can't do that. But you know, that's why I can't see anybody broke in this town. There's always something to do."

It is usually the same people, the same young men, on the Avenue during the afternoons and evenings. Many have known the area for a lifetime. Only a couple of years ago thirteen of them could be found on the side street, halfway up the hill, at their own club, a tenement basement, in a building that no longer stands. It was different from the Guyamo Social Club, the poolroom where they now hang out. They were members, not patrons. And they formed bonds based on equal parts of hope and desperation. The hope is diminished now and the bonds are between men, no longer boys. A stocky, tall black in his early twenties steps out from the noise and crowding of the poolroom. Standing in the doorway he takes several deep breaths and offers a disarmingly soft smile to an old man hurrying through the evening toward the bus stop. In the days when the real club was open up on the hill, he was the one, the member most often looked to by the others for answers and decisions. His throaty voice still keeps things cool, but the ardor of the old days is gone.

"When we had the club in the basement, you know, everybody lived right in the block. You just stayed. You'd go upstairs in the morning, take your bath, do what your mother wanted you to—you know, do things around the house you had to do for your mother. When you finished it was right back downstairs again. We had everything there. A record player, television, playing cards—anything you wanted to do was just about there. We had the whole basement from front to back. We had one, two, three, about four big rooms and a long hallway plus the rooms in the back where we kept the dogs and stuff. Our Doberman,

the biggest dog, he got killed just a couple of weeks ago. The guy who had him was down on the street and he got hit by a cab. He was old anyway, about nine. That was that. All together, you know, with the mother and father we had twenty-seven puppies off and on. They was good watch dogs. We gave most of 'em to friends. We got Brandy, the father, from Poppo, who used to live across the street. We got him because Poppo was scared of him. We figured that we had room in the basement, in the club, and that he wouldn't bite nobody too much. Just about everybody in the club was scared of him. We voted. It was an honest vote and the ones that were really scared of him just had to put up with him. They lost. But I never was scared. He was always good to me, you know, maybe because I treated him right. I used to take him out a lot. Take him to Central Park for six, seven hours. I'd be so tired he'd have to bring me home. You know, that was a good time. We met a lot of people in that block. We used to give dances in the club on the weekends. People used to come from all over the city, you know, people we never knew. We used to put our posters in the schools and projects and stuff. We had a lot of people. We always made people welcome. You know, they'd come and we'd say, 'Hey, you here again this weekend! Glad to see your face,' you know, stuff like that. Give 'em a drink, you know, people that came all the time, regulars, we'd give 'em a drink. We'd make 'em feel like, you know, the same way a bar does. You go in a bar all the time, they might give you one or two on the house 'cause you're spending your money. You come every week and spend your money, once in a while you want to

36

come in and, you know, let the people say that they appreciate your
being there. A lot of times we used
to give freebies, you know. We'd
take money out of the treasury and
go out and buy a whole lot of food.
Then let the people in for free, let
them eat the food for free. We'd give
a freebie one night so that the next
week when we gave one for money
people'd come. We figured the other
weekends they don't mind payin' because they'd figure we ain't makin'
that much money. They'd say, 'At
least they did appreciate us comin'.
They gave us something free.'

"Once in a while we used to get a
couple of dudes that came in, you
know, want to tear up the place. People get jealous so they want to tear
up your place. We always talked it
down, we didn't have too many
fights. We had a few, you know, different ones got into a little fight
sometimes but that was a last resort.
Sometimes we'd get the kind of guy
that wants to sneak in. 'I paid.'
'Who you pay?' 'I paid such and
such.' 'He wasn't at the door when
you come around.' We'd round up
the whole club. 'Well, point out
which one you paid.' He couldn't
point him out and it couldn't be
someone else 'cause these were the
only members of the club. We'd
charge fifty cents, seventy-five
cents, a dollar, you know. We'd
figure what was right for that
weekend. Most drinks were sixty
cents but we charged seventy-five
for Scotch. We had dinners. We used
to have the girls, you know, they
liked to hang around, and we'd have
them cook dinners, things like ham
and collard greens. We'd charge like
a dollar for dinner. You figure you
party, you drink a little, maybe
smoke a little reefer, then you get
hungry. So we made pretty good

money off the food. We used to go uptown to the Spanish market and for about thirteen dollars we'd get a nice-size ham. Figure we made more than that off cuttin' it. We'd make our money back because, you know, after everyone got high they didn't realize that half the time they wasn't eating everything. You know, they'd just eat a little bit for a dollar. Lots of times we'd go to other parties and the party'd get over early. We'd bring the crowd to ours. Go searchin', you know. We might go to a party and there's some dudes, and people'd say 'Ohhh, we came to this place for nothin'.' We'd tell 'em, 'Well, come down to our place in an hour's time.' And we'd rush back and hook up the place real good and the next thing you know here comes the crowd. Our business was word of mouth, you know, by travelin'. We made out pretty good. We used to make like three hundred dollars a weekend. Like in one weekend we made enough to buy our club jackets. They cost three hundred and eighty some dollars. Sometimes we'd put on our jackets and just walk through blocks, you know, just advertising. We never ran into too much trouble. Once in a while, if somebody was alone and had the jacket on, and went past a gang, the gang would try to make you wear your jacket inside out. That was like an insult, if you take off your jacket and turn it. You're never supposed to turn your jacket inside out.

But we wasn't a gang club, we was a social club. But the gang clubs, they figure you belong to a clique or something, so four or five guys would get around you and tell you to turn your jacket while you're in their territory. A couple of the guys,

they turned their jackets, but nobody ever made me turn mine. We wasn't out fightin' or nothin', we was out just tryin' to make a little money and have a good time because we had a basement.

"Sometimes we used to rent the club out to people that had, you know, birthdays and things like that. We'd charge 'em something to use the club and then we'd just, like, watch over 'cause this was ours. They would give us the right to let in maybe each club member and the member's girl. Then during the days we used to let the little kids from the block come down. We used to show them movies. You know, go out and buy a whole lot of popcorn and stuff, pretzels, and let the little kids come in. We'd charge 'em a nickel or a dime and show movies. We had a projector and a screen and we used to have, like, a whole lot of Three Stooges movies, Popeyes, you know, all the cartoons and stuff. It made the little kids feel good. It's just that they wanted to see what was inside the door. Sayin', 'Well, y'all hangin' out down there, let us see.' So we let 'em in, you know, to make the people see that we wasn't doin' nothin' wrong. Because the kids would go upstairs and say, 'Momma, we was down in the club today and we seen such and such.' The parents say, 'Oh, they let you down in there?' They hear the kids talkin', the kids don't say they seen nothin' goin' on wrong so it made the parents feel like, 'Hey, maybe they are doin' something right,' you know. It was nice. I really liked it. If we kept it long enough we was gonna try and get our funds together and organize trips during the summer. Rent a couple of buses for the kids and take 'em to Bear Mountain, or something. But I

guess things started shakin' up so it never got to that point, you know, where we could do it. But we used to talk about it. We'd have our regular meetings and talk about different things we wanted to do, you know, after we got ourselves established, and was really makin' money. But the buildings started comin' down and when you got thirteen people for members you got thirteen different ideas. And there were other problems and family problems. A lot of things you talk about never come off, you know. But if it would've lasted from then to now I think a lot of things might have been different, you know . . ."

"When I get up in the morning now I usually sit around my house, my grandmother's apartment. I read a little bit, listen to the radio, you know, read a book and maybe make a couple of phone calls to see what I'm gonna do when I do come out. Then, maybe two or three o'clock I'll come downstairs for a while. I'll take a walk through the neighborhood, stop in the candy store to see if anyone's there, stop in the club if it's open. If nobody's out yet I just hang around or sometimes I say to myself, 'Well, I'll take a walk uptown to my mother's house.' By the time I visit her awhile and come back, usually somebody's out. Sometimes when nobody's around I go to the movies or something, you know. Different days I try to do a different thing. I try not to do the same thing every day.

"When I hang out I hang out for a while, then in the evenin' time everybody makes their move, you know. Some go home, some go this way, you know, whichever you feel you want to do. It's about three years now since I've had a full-time job. A few guys work. They work until they lose their job and they try to find another job. But most of the guys here ain't workin' I don't think. A few still go to school so that takes up most of their day, you know. Everybody gets a little money from where they can. Like you might get yours from your mother, this guy gets his from here, you know. They come with whatever they got. So if you figure if you got a couple of dollars, somebody else got a couple of dollars, you know, intertwine it together, stretch it and it goes a long way. Share a bottle, split up a few beers. Dollar here, dollar there, you know. But most times you figure we'll be in the poolroom. It's a quarter for a game of pool. You might put one quarter in and win all night. So it's not too expensive."

"Things changed here a lot. It went down, the buildings went, the same people aren't here now. We still come back here, but I mean, you know, the older people that was in the neighborhood, different people, they're gone. It was a big change, you know, it's just not the same atmosphere no more. The environment changed, there's not any closeness. Like when we were up on the street everyone was like a family, almost. Spanish, white, black, they was all like a big community. You always was doin' things. It was maybe trips, or when they painted the lot we had it to go into. It was, you know, a knitted thing. Where, you know, you might have known someone and you'd see them and say, 'How you feelin' this morning, how's your mother,' things like that. Now the majority of the people that was in the block, the older ones, they moved. You don't see them and you don't see their kids or nothin' no more. All that we see are ourselves, the ones who come back to hang out. The older people that are left, they don't have that closeness no more, you know. Like, now when they see you they speak because maybe they know you or sometimes they speak because they don't recognize you and they're scared. There's none of that where you feel like, 'Hey, everything's okay,' you know.

"I can sense when a person's a little fearful, you know. I notice it everywhere I go. I notice it in my own building. Lots of times when I get on the elevator the people who were waiting to get on, won't get on, you know. But it doesn't bother me because I feel maybe if I was older I'd feel the same way. People in the street, like, if you walk by them, and it's evening, and you're mindin' your business, just walkin', they might be in front of you. They turn real quick soon as they hear your footsteps. But I guess that's a mental thing, you know, from readin' the paper. The *Daily News* plays up so much crime that they hear about it all the time. It's that even if they ain't fearful, they're fearful, you know. Their mind plays a trick on them. It don't really bother me 'cause I know I'm not out there doin' nothin' to nobody. So who am I to tell them that I'm not doin' anything because the next guy that comes might be the mugger or the robber. So I feel that if that's their way to protect themselves, by being fearful, let 'em do it. That's their thing. It's not really botherin' me. I just go. I look at it and say to myself, 'Why? Because I'm black they feel this way?' but that's their thing. Let them do what they want."

The buildings, determined stone memories of a time when the city was adding to itself and growing, always growing, have owners. Most of the structures, nearing the beginning of their second century, are owned and ignored by faceless realty corporations and banks. A few are even the property of the city, given up and over by landlords who drew a bottom line on their investments and accepted an end to years of small profits. But there are still some tenements owned by people who have names and presences. The landlord can still tell stories of his flight from Germany in the thirties, the hard and bitter work to get established in the trade in the city, and the determination to own a building, any building, so that his small wholesaling operation wouldn't be at the mercy of another landlord. He sweeps the sidewalk each morning, keeps the hallways painted, and oversees the tenants; five or six white couples who fill his apartments for a few years, to save money, and then to pass them on to others on the way through.

"Chester was the super for a building at the end of the block. He worked for me at the same time. For me and also Mrs. Finkle. He quit. He was pretty good for me, Chester, but my tenants didn't like him very much. As a matter of fact nobody liked him. Oh yeah, he was a thief too. But I let him steal. He didn't ask for too much money for the job so I could go along with it. So if he steals a pair of shoes, a jacket once in a while, I let him be happy. If I call a plumber today the plumber wants, for a small job, up to one hundred and fifty dollars. And Chester, I watched him and he did certain kinds of work to my satisfaction.

But I couldn't let him alone. So now he has disappeared altogether.

"One thing that makes it bad for the neighborhood is that the city rented a building for the Welfare. They come at five-thirty and they line up, in the morning. Standing in hallways, having their breakfast. Paper cups in the street. There are garbage cans but they wouldn't throw paper cups in the garbage cans, no, it has to be in the street. So how can we educate these people?

"Before, we had only in the neighborhood Germans, Italians. And now Puerto Ricans are coming in. It was about five years ago that those people started coming in. The landlords didn't care much for the buildings. We had colored supers and they tried to bring in their people. There aren't many kids around here anymore, just across the street. I chase them away or I call the police. I don't want them dirtying up the sidewalks or spraying up my walls. If they would behave I wouldn't mind but it's a rough element. Spanish and colored. It's not pleasant.

"The kids . . . they play ball against the front of the building, I can't make a telephone call. They roller-skate on the sidewalk. They just pick my place because I keep it clean. It's the same with the dogs. People have dogs and they do their droppings just in front of the building. Right on the sidewalk. As soon as I call the precinct, the police respond quickly, very quickly. I tell them that there are too many children gathering in front of my place, that they don't belong on my side of the street. I ask the police to please disperse them, clean 'em up. And a few minutes later a squad car comes and they clean up. It's very delicate.

I don't want to be involved with those people. If you play too rough they might kill you. They could stick a knife in your back. So it's a beautiful thing that the police do. You have to be careful. But it's worth it. I thought about retiring to Florida. I went down there and it's nice for a few days, but then I'd had enough. Then I came back again to the city. I like to see action. I like to be where the action is. Subways, people, maybe aggravation, excitement. Because it's the best. It's the only place, it's the only place, to my way of thinking."

The Oasis

"We'll take friends out to the garden and they'll say, 'Oh, this reminds me of Paris, or of Rome.' And my husband had some clients from the Midwest over a couple of months ago. We had lunch set up in the garden and they looked around and said, 'Gosh, this looks just like Pierre, South Dakota.' "

—A RESIDENT

It is a street of homes. And the focus of the people who live in the carefully maintained four-story structures is away from the tree-shaded street, and back into cloistered yards and gardens. The houses were built for merchants in the days when having household help meant a staff of servants, not just an occasional cleaning woman. The houses are large, and since few modern owners need a floor or a floor-and-a-half for a staff, second homes—extensive duplex apartments—have been created. These have become the rented residences for young families who, in a few years, can be expected to purchase their own town houses.

The avenues, which enclose the block, like gaudy mass-produced bookends, show the wear and muted promise of a modern city. But the street and several parallel streets, both above and below, have managed, through the involvement of residents who know and can dial the right phone numbers, to retain a justified feeling of permanence. The location, in the heart of the commercial city, means convenience, easy access to the big stores, to big offices, to theaters, the major restaurants—convenience and access without sacrificing a sense of personal space and private existence. The area is not composed only of superlatives. While there are "important" restaurants, there are also small places, quiet places. And there are shops, groceries, drugstores, even hardware stores where odd-size washers can be located in badly labeled bins. This makes a difference to a woman possessing the familiar look of fashion-magazine cover subjects.

"The night I came home with the baby from the hospital, my mother had arrived to help, but there hadn't been time to do any shopping. I called my husband at his office and asked if he could bring home some food. He said, 'Don't worry. I'll take care of it.' He called the little French restaurant down near the corner, and said, 'My wife just came home from the hospital with a new baby and we don't have any dinner, and I know that you don't normally do any take-out service, but could I come and get something to take home?' And the woman at the restaurant said, 'What time would you like dinner?' He told her nine, and at a quarter to nine our doorbell rang. There at the door was a waiter, all dressed in white, with a big silver tray. He sat us down at the table, served us our dinner, and left. And about an hour later the doorbell rang again and there he was with the silver tray and chocolate mousses for dessert. Then he cleared all the dishes and left. It was fantastic! The owner came by at the end, herself, to make certain that everything was all right. And the incredible thing is that we had never even been there before. It's not like we were great regular customers. They just heard that someone in the neighborhood had had a baby and they wanted to help out. It was really terrific."

Gestures, acts of civility, and proffered friendship bind people together as neighbors, if not lasting friends. But there are, of course, other, less positive acts. And when, unannounced, a challenge to a style of living and a collective sense of well-being is offered, regardless of an area's economic level, reactions are bound to be heard. It can start with something as taken-for-granted as a tree.

"We were having brunch in the dining room. And out the window we saw two men climbing up the tree. They had ropes hanging down, that sort of thing, and I remember I took our son upstairs to get a better view. It was just a few weeks before his third birthday. Anyway, we were standing at the upstairs window, my wife was still down in the dining room, and the whole thing went from the extreme of waving to the men and saying, 'Oh, look at the man in the tree,' and our son waving and saying, 'Hi Mister Man, hi Mister Tree,' and everybody laughing and the tree men waving back, to wanting to throw axes at them a couple of hours later. But that's the way it started. Sort of a very nice, friendly thing. Two men were going to prune the tree."

No one is certain just how long the tree has been standing. But no one remembers a time when it wasn't there, the most stately of the several trees spaced throughout adjoining backyards. The neighborhood tree association, a ten-dollar-a-year membership collective, doesn't keep such records. Instead, it uses its income to maintain the street-side trees, and plants and carefully nurtures beds of flowers at the tree bases. The association also offers its services in caring for any backyard trees that prove to be too much for a homeowner. The young mother who had prepared a leisurely Sunday brunch had joined the association soon after she and her family moved into the upper two floors of the house.

"It was really sad. I mean it had to be one of the largest willows within fifty miles of the city. It was one of the major reasons that we took this place, and when you think about the people who own this house—they have four sons, every one of them played in the backyard from the time they were infants. Cutting the tree was like cutting off part of their heritage, their whole life. When I saw that the men up in the tree weren't just lightly pruning it but were slashing away at major limbs, I called my friend downstairs and said, 'What are they doing to the tree?' 'Oh, don't worry,' she said. 'The doctor next door said he was just having some trimming done.' She said that he had asked if the tree pruners could come in through her house and use the backyard. The main part of the trunk is in the doctor's yard, but the roots have grown through and the tree mostly overhangs this yard. Anyway, within just a few minutes you could see that the men were cutting off major sections of the tree. You could hear the limbs crashing down and you could hear the ladies from the buildings out back—a couple of buildings there have small apartments and a number of old women live in them— you could hear them crying out each time a branch was cut down. My husband and I were horrified, watching, and I called downstairs again and I said, 'They aren't trimming the tree,' and she said, 'I know it now. I know they're not.' She went out into

the yard and shouted at the men to stop, but they didn't seem to understand or speak English. The doctor was standing up on his roof watching the whole thing, so our landlord got up on our roof to try to talk to him, to stop it. But he wouldn't listen to reason at all. That's when the police were called.

"I think two or three squad cars pulled up—they got here pretty fast —and the landlord told them he wanted the tree men stopped. All their ropes and equipment, the whole base of operations, was in this yard. And, I mean, the men even fell out of the tree a couple of times, right into the yard. They just weren't tree surgeons—my husband says they were tree hit-men—and their truck out on the street didn't say anything about tree surgery, it said 'Refuse Removal.' And that's what they were, refuse people. When the police arrived, people were still at their windows up and down the yards, shouting, and you could hear crying. It was very, very upsetting. I mean, I had never seen anybody deface anything like that. It was just so beautiful before they started cutting. But at any rate the police told the men that they should leave, that there had been arguments over this tree for years and they shouldn't get involved in it. And when the men said that they had been hired by the doctor to cut it down, the landlord told them that if they ever came back he would press charges and have them arrested. The doctor, of course, disappeared when the police came. But, you know, the men did try to come back a week or two later, and they tried to cut it from the doctor's side of the fence. But they couldn't do it. They kept falling over the fence. And the police came

again. When the thing was all over the doctor called various people in the neighborhood and accused them of harassing his tree surgeons and making it impossible to do a proper job. He said that that was the reason that the tree was scarred. And that man, he doesn't even live here. He just uses the building for his medical offices. He lives out somewhere in the suburbs. I called him and talked to him and he was absolutely foul on the telephone. And I told him what I thought, you know, of him —that he had no respect for his neighbors and no feeling for the city, and then, I mean, I really lost my cool.

"The whole thing was terrible and now just a little more than half of the tree is still standing. But because of the neighbors' reaction, and the tree association—they wrote him a letter—I don't think there'll be any more trouble. It's unusual for anything like this to happen here. People here do care about their homes and they seem to care, or at least be really considerate of the other people on the street. But there are always aberrations, I guess, and the doctor fills that role. But it's a minor role."

A Block

The first-floor faces of most of the six- and seven-story tenement buildings were painted during a six-hour rush. There was a need to hurry, for a concert was scheduled to start at seven o'clock in the evening—the block was going to be ready. And by the time the big band and its famous leader began playing their distinctive Latin music the stones glistened with white, brilliant red, deep blue, and rich green coverings. When the poverty-program worker, employed by the district's publicly financed poverty corporation, made the turn from the park-flanking avenue into his own block, the crowd had swelled to nearly five hundred people. The orchestra, scheduled and paid for within the guidelines of a city summer program, made and accepted contact with the audience and gave them the brazen, powerfully themed music of sunbaked villages and rain forests. The poverty worker, who had gained his job after being laid off as a longshoreman, had spent several earlier days locating landlords and the neighborhood's small shopkeepers and suggesting that they donate the paint and brushes for the block decorating. And now the street had a festive sparkle, and any unexpressed doubts could be put away for a few hours. At the edge of the crowd three brothers, the oldest seventeen, the youngest thirteen, listened intently. The evening was good, the music terrific. It was quite different from an afternoon several months earlier when the fourteen-year-old middle brother had watched a different kind of production on the block.

"I went home about one o'clock in the afternoon to eat. And when I came out again, about three o'clock, this man, he was white, he came

"More people hang around and work and play in this block than I've seen in any other block. We must have eight hundred families here, mostly PRs, a lotta old people, colored, and a lotta kids. It's a block known for kids. It's a good damn block."

—A POVERTY-PROGRAM WORKER

53

around the corner and starts down the block, you know, walking calmly step by step. And as he was walking I was standing in the doorway and I saw three guys behind him, three black dudes walkin' behind him. You know, I didn't think they were going to mug him on the block in front of anybody. But then they start running and they grabbed him, you know, one stays out to guard to see if anybody's gonna do anything. Another grabs him and the other one's trying to get his hand to the wallet, you know, to get the wallet. And then the man starts screaming. So one of the dudes, you know, hits him in the jaw, but he's still struggling to get away. There were like five or ten ladies out there hollering, 'Get the police . . . when we need the police they're never here,' and stuff like that. They were screaming all along, but, you know, they can't do nothing so they just kept on screaming, 'Get the police, get the police!' and all that stuff. And then these three other guys, they were on the stoop in the middle of the block. They didn't see it but, you know, they heard the people screamin' and they came up to see what was happening. When the three colored guys saw them coming, you know, they hit the man one more time and they ripped almost the whole side of his pants off trying for the wallet. And then they started to run. And the guys from the stoop, you know, they picked up some cans and bottles and started throwin' them at these guys. But they jumped the block and cut into the park. Then after that the police came. But I know if those guys from the stoop had got there in time they would have helped the man. . . . They did make them run. And I

guess the muggers thought the man was known on the block and maybe we were going to help him. In the beginning they probably thought that no one was going to help so they took their time.

"The newspapers exaggerated because they took the news from the man that got mugged, and he exaggerated a lot. He said there were over a hundred people there watching. That doesn't make sense 'cause there was about ten women and some little kids, I'd say about twenty-five altogether. Not a hundred, or even close to that number. And the man said that he didn't hear a sound of anyone trying to help him. That doesn't make sense either because it took a long time for them to get the wallet out and all the while the women were screaming for the police. And those little kids couldn't do anything, and those guys from the block, I saw them comin' from the stoop to help. And those black dudes . . . when they saw those guys coming, that's when they really started, you know, getting into some action. That's when they just punched the guy quickly and then just ripped off the pants. The man told the newspapers that he was surprised that they didn't pull a knife or something on him. Well, that's probably 'cause they saw those guys from the block comin'. I mean he could've been hurt a lot worse. The man should have thought back before he said that, and he should have said that it was little kids and ladies out there. And he should have mentioned the little help-out that the guys from the block gave him, you know, instead of sayin' there was a hundred not helpin'. But I can understand it. Maybe he didn't see those three

and they both happened when there was nobody on the block. I mean no men around, people who could get involved. That's on the weekdays. But on the weekends, they'll catch 'em. You know, the guys'll be going down to the gym and they'll be out and you got the men around, you know. They'll try and help out. They'll say, 'We're after you, let him go!' And they'll chase after them. Because, you know, on our block we try to keep things quiet. People try to keep crime away from the block. Anyway, after that happened on the block that afternoon I stood there to see what would happen and then I went over to the playground to shoot some baskets. And about two hours later I was sittin' on the playground benches. And I just looked across the street and there was this parcel post truck. And all of a sudden this unmarked car came by and stopped right in front of it. And people started gathering around and traffic started getting heavier, you know. So I went to the fence and I said, 'Something's happening over there.' So we walked across the street and somebody said that a guy had just gotten stabbed. Everything was so quick! First the guy got stabbed, the unmarked car came by, traffic got heavy, the guys got away. I never seen so much action in one day! . . . When those two events happened that day, I felt so, you know, funny. First it was some black guys to a white person, then it was three Spanish guys to a black guy. And I say, 'How can they do this?' That's why it's so bad around here. People want to get together. But how's that gonna be? Muggings almost every day. Killing their own race and themselves, that's no way to get together. There's too much

guys come off the stoop. That's probably the way he felt because he was just worried about the guys trying to mug him, not nobody else, so he wouldn't hear nothing, I don't think. Like the time I had a fight my brother told me there was a lot of screamin' goin' on but I didn't hear nothin'. You're too worried about the guy hitting you, you know, you're just worried about that. He probably did whatever he could to, you know, try to keep them from gettin' into his pockets. But I don't think he realized what the guys from the block were doin' to help. He probably thought that they were just coming by, that they didn't mind, and that they'd let him get mugged, you know. But not the guys from our block, they wouldn't do that. There's only two muggings on our block that I can remember

mugging. And police can't stop that because they can't stop all the dealers selling dope. First they got to catch all the dealers and even before that they got to catch the way it's comin' in here. With all their crime-detecting equipment I can't understand why they can't find out where the dope's coming from. I don't get off on narcotics, even when they're offered to me. I just walk away. I would say about ten times I'd be comin' out of the gym and guys would say, 'Want a blow of this stuff?' And I'd say, 'A blow of what?' And he says, 'Some of this stuff.' And I'd say, 'No, man, you can keep it for all I care.' And these other guys say, 'Let me have a nickel, man.' And I say, 'For what?' And they say, 'So I can buy a bag of shit and I'll give you some, man.' And I say, 'Here's a nickel but you can keep the stuff.' You know, friends like that I don't need. I mean, they can be friends but they wouldn't be true friends. They'll be friends if you join them or if you lend them a nickel or if you do what they do. The only way I'm gonna get stuck on narcotics is if somebody stuffs it in me. And if they do I'm goin' straight to the hospital. Or they'd have to have a gun at my throat because, you know, I think it's better to die by a shooting than to die of an OD. If you get shot you're gonna suffer, but not as much as if you OD. That's one thing I can live without. I was talkin' to this guy one time, I forget his name, but he was a dope addict, you know. And he was sayin', 'I better cut this shit out, man, I'm doin' bad.' And I said, 'How long you been on it?' And he said, 'About eight months.' And I said, 'The only way you can stop is goin' through that cold turkey, or

goin' to a program. That way they'll give it to you but not as much.' And he says, 'Ah no, man, I can't do that, I can't do that.' That's gotta be pretty bad to have that feeling of wanting to do it again and again. You know my sister's boyfriend is in a drug program. And I'm not ashamed to say this about him because he was a junkie but he's been tryin' hard and I think he's gonna make it. Like, my sister said to him, 'Either you have the dope or you have me. Now if you want the dope you can have it and I'll forget about you. Or you can forget the dope and stay with me.' He chose her. Now he's in a program and he's gonna make it."

For a few weeks after the "mugging," the incident and the block were referred to frequently in the newspapers and mentioned on the radio talk shows as an example of city cruelty, the jungle that waits "out there" for the "good citizens." But the block maintained its own pace with vitality, some young dreams, some laughter, and music, and tragedies—certainly some tragedies. For life is lived here as it is without any great variation throughout the Hispanic-dominated, publicly assisted district. Most of the people have been on the block for a long time, two or three years at least, and two or three years is a long time in under-serviced, crowded buildings. And there are few if any residents who, if a choice were offered, would choose to stay on the block. But that reality doesn't make it any less than, as the poverty worker says, "A damn good block. Sure, we have some trouble, but there are people who do try to take care of things, take care of the little kids. And like

the people who worked painting the buildings, just about everybody around that could put a hand in, did. My biggest personal problem is with my apartment. My wife and I got a man that lives on top of us that's careless. It's because of him that we get water leaking. We get water coming down from upstairs constantly. Now, that's because the guy fills up his bathtub, he stands in the bathroom, and he dives in. I mean it, I got paneling in our house, we got our place all fixed up and then there's this guy that jumps from his bathroom door into his bathtub. I mean, what the hell does he think he's got, a pool? He's probably our biggest problem, and then the rats, the roaches, the whole block seems to be getting them bad, I guess because the garbage isn't getting picked up as often as it should be."

The concert, originally scheduled to last for three hours, continued with only brief breaks until shortly before midnight. The three brothers held their ground, listened, beat out rhythms, talked with friends and made several trips to the "iced slush" stand set up for the evening at the corner. And as the members of the band packed up their instruments and sound equipment, the brothers watched under the dim street lights from the top step of their stoop. The oldest brother spoke of moving:

"My mother plans on movin' again but it's hard to find good places. Sometimes the places look nice from the outside but, you know, sometimes the apartments don't have any heat or hot water, or sometimes the radiator don't work, or whatever. And my mother can't be wastin' time. She has to take time from work because she won't go if it's gettin' dark. Because the block may be nice, but there may be a junkie or two, you find junkies everywhere you go. But she wants to get away from almost everything. She don't want to be scared, you know. She wants to live where if she had a back door she don't have to have a gate to lock out the robbers. And there's only one way you can be like that and that's to move to the country. Up there they leave the car windows wide open, keys, you know, in the ignition. It's unbelievable! And if you leave your house windows open, the only thing you have to worry about comin' in up there are the mosquitos."

Neutral Ground

On the surface the area survives in a time that no longer exists, not even in fantasy. It is where things were created—works of art, literature, drama, music, entire intellectual movements, or so the stories, the endless stories, told and retold in small, stained bars, would have it. A nearly characterless bar is remembered by a pretelevision generation as the place where Dylan Thomas began his final alcohol-triggered spasms, which ended with his premature death. And in the corner, over by the window, Brendan Behan came off the wagon, irrevocably. Sweet blues, raucous gut-bucket dixieland, harmonied folk-sounds used to filter through the doors of dimly lit bars and nightclubs. And the attitude, the atmosphere if not the product, lingers. The comfortable proportions of nineteenth-century residences cast an aura of sturdy casualness on the people who live there. Names, if not the works of the names, are remembered now in restaurant neon and on occasional small, patinaed plaques that are invisible to all but the seekers. The whirlwind is difficult to locate. But comfortable, studied living is available and enjoyed. And there are people of all cuts who are determined to at least stay within the area's constantly fluctuating boundaries as long as they remain in the city. It is a district, and personal identification comes from the extended environs. A young bank executive explains his attachment and the attachment of his designer wife to an attitude:

"The first place I lived here was over by the Square, next to the law school dormitory. I had only a quasi-view of the park. I think the reason I moved there was a certain

"This is a small town, really, within the city. And it's very different. People walk, they walk all around. They stop in places for a few minutes, have a cup of coffee, have a drink, go to another place. It's not bar-hopping, it's just going around to see people."

—A TELEVISION PRODUCER

amount of character in the area, and also there were some interesting people that you got to know by being there. I mean, every time I walked down the block somebody was out either sweeping the sidewalks or plastering gummed stickers on windows of illegally parked cars. There really was a group of fanatic people there trying to protect their environment—and it wasn't easy because the city had taken over five hotels around the park for welfare clients. What happened to the whole street was that what started out as a

place of character and interest turned in less than two years into a tourist trap, a hang-out. All kinds of people came down there. It turned into another amusement park. And the next street turned, it deteriorated from the café night-spot area into just a fast-food junk-shop type of thing. I still think I probably would have stayed if it hadn't been for my bike. I kept my bike parked outside, with a massive chain on it. I came down one afternoon and there were two little fellows sitting there with a hacksaw, going at the chain. I said, 'What the hell are you doing? That's my bike.' So they got up and walked away. I went around the corner and then I came back and they were right there again, hacking away. Well, I chased one of them and when I caught up with him I looked around and there were no police, nothing, and he just stood there looking at me. The only way I could get him was by attacking, and I was not about to do that. So we looked at each other for a minute or so and then we walked away from each other. I came back, got the bike, took it inside and chained it to a railing in the hallway. And two weeks later the bike was gone. There wasn't even any subtlety in the whole thing. No style. At any rate that particular area had deteriorated in less than two years as a place for living, so we moved. I said, 'We'll spend some money to reduce the hassles,' and we moved about ten blocks west to this apartment.

"One of the reasons we like this area and want to stay here is that most of the people I know in business live uptown. And down here we effectively isolate ourselves and can have our own life. We do know people in the shops—it's that kind of

neighborhood. We know the cleaner and he knows us. It's that people here have time for you, it's just not so hassled as uptown. Shopkeepers, merchants—obviously they're here to make money but they don't seem so grabby about it. They're nice to customers and if they don't have something, they'll order it or they'll say next week we'll have it or something like that. There's another thing, too. I love living close to the street—I just don't like apartment buildings, high-rises. And I think there's something valuable in being close to the street, to hear the noise of the street, to hear people, to be able to get to the street. And it gives an identification with the city. You know, there's one phenomenon that we have noticed in the three years we've been in this apartment. That's the rise of the gay culture. Maybe they were always here but the overt display of hand-holding and everything—it's become characteristic of the area. Most of them seem all right but then you do get the leather guys. But I think all in all I consider it positive because they're harmless. And I would rather see them than some other type, they're no real street menace.

"One thing I heard a lot about when we first came to the area was how politically active and aware the people are. That's part of the myth. I don't sense it at all. As an observer I think that the people who run politics or are involved in politics are freaks. There doesn't seem to be any normal, average, everyday, decent citizen involved in the process of making community decisions. It's either a rabid freak or an individual who has some kind of a problem. With a terrific drive for power or job frustration. They're nuts in some way, driven out into this chaotic arena. The regular people of the city —and I believe there are some, the average guys—are not heard. I think the average guy is someone who has a home, who lives here, who goes to work and comes home and goes shopping. And if someone asks him what his views are about the community, he says, 'These are my views,' and if someone comes by and says, 'Joe, you gotta get excited about this issue because they're going to move a McDonald's hamburger stand in next to you and your property value is going to drop —you have to get excited,' then he goes out and sits in on a meeting and listens for a while and signs his name to a petition. But in the end he walks away totally helpless, because he can't really do anything. He can't really do anything about what is happening around him. There will be weeks of having leaflets pushed under doors every day, and come-here, go-there, and suddenly there will be nothing. Whatever was going to happen will happen and nothing more will be heard. A few leaders have flexed muscles and made their own trade-offs, their careers are improved, and everybody else is used as fodder."

The district is cut by streets and avenues and dented by alleys, mews, courts, and places. It is the small spaces, the enclosures, that are perhaps the most prized by residents —for, in addition to the privacy that is offered by a house-lined street, there is the added confidence that comes with a gate, setting the walkways off as something special and semiprivate. A producer-writer found his home, his first city apartment, through the kind of accident that occurs often enough to be considered not unusual.

"About five years ago, when I came back from living and going to school in Boston, my mother, she's a psychologist, she volunteered to help me find a place. We looked in the papers and we walked around the area and finally I said, 'Let's try some brokers.' So we walked into a real estate office. The broker, a woman, was there and she looked at my mother and said, 'Don't I know you?' My mother said, 'I'm sorry, I don't know your name.' The woman introduced herself and said that ten or fifteen years before she had called up, she had found the listing in the phone book, and said that her friend was in trouble. She thought she might kill herself. And my mother had met her friend and treated her and everything worked out well. Then the woman said, 'What do you want?' I said, 'I want an apartment, real cheap, great big, old, atmosphere . . .' She said, 'Well I can't do everything but I'll try.' Then, twenty-four hours later she gave me a choice of two places and I chose this, the studio with French windows overlooking a garden, kitchen, good closets, and a working fireplace. I've been here ever since.

"There are people here, on the court, who've been around for twenty and thirty years. Writers, editors, people involved in show business. A lot of them seem to be book people, they came here a long time ago when they were in their heyday. In the back there's an enormous garden, and just to the left a schoolyard, and trees—enormous old trees—and bushes and shrubs and people are always out there planting things. The woman on my floor, the only other apartment on the second floor, has been here for at least fifteen years. She's a writer who no one except students of English literature has ever heard about. But she's a cult figure. And there are always people ringing her bell but she never lets any of them in. We have fights all the time because, as she says, she doesn't want anyone involved in her personal life. I don't want anything to do with it. Like one time I opened my door and there's this guy coming up the stairs. He was walking on all fours and he was wearing a tie and a tee shirt. I just kind of stared at him and he passed me by and went to the cult figure's door, scratched at it, it opened, and he went in. In less than a minute he came out, still on his hands and knees, with a bucket of water, and starts scrubbing the floors. I went back into my apartment and got ready to go to bed. And about half an hour later I heard scratching on my door. So I went to the door, opened it, and there was this guy cleaning my door. He was washing the front of my door. And the cult figure sticks her head out of her door and says, 'You're so dirty! You have such a dirty door. Can't you keep it clean?' I closed my door and tried to go to sleep. It wasn't easy, with all the guilt about keeping a dirty door. The guy above me is about fifty years old and looks about thirty. He wears leather all the time, rides a motorcycle. He used to have a baby grand in his apartment, and it's a small apartment, but he had an accident on his motorcycle so he figured he'd better get rid of the piano because he can't play it the way he wants to. Anyway, he's always in leather. He belongs to one of those clubs downtown, leather clubs, motorcycle clubs. And he and the cult figure haven't talked to each other in the last fifteen years. Sometimes the people seem a little bizarre but it's just—it's their home, and they're settled in and now what are they going to do. They're stuck, in a sense. The guy who shares the floor with the leather guy is the guy I call the 'Mystery Man.' I've been here five years and I've seen him ten times. We're very cordial, we had a drink once, we talk. He's a traveling salesman for some big clothing company and he's lived here for probably twenty years. But he's never here! He comes in at four in the morning and leaves at eight. Occasionally he's home for two or three days, like maybe once every year or so. He used to have a woman come in to just pick up his laundry because he was never there when the laundry was open. She'd pick it up, take it, take care of it, you know, and then deliver it. I think there's only one complete family in the whole court. Everyone else is either like a divorced woman with her daughter, single people, or gay couples, but there are no real families—straight couples and kids—none of that. The gays aren't the affected gays, they're very cool about it, quiet, you know. No one is hiding anything but no one is showy.

"I think that the area is about the most alive area in the city. And yet there isn't any street fear. Lots of people are out on the streets. There has always been a late-night crowd. And I have found very little crime. There are rip-offs all the time but nothing violent, not a lot of violence. And neighborhood people, when an issue comes up, are pretty together about fighting it—whether it's a highway or street lamps. It really is kind of a small town. You can get services here, things repaired. There are people who will do things for you, and it's very, very friendly. You can get anything you need and still be free to exist in your own world, I mean, I can be alone without being isolated. I remember the first time it snowed in the winter. It was beautiful and I opened the windows—it was freezing but I opened the windows—and just looked out. The snow, all this snow, was covering the trees and the yard and it was quiet. One of the kids from the court was out there playing with snowballs . . . it was fantastic."

Gray Neighborhood

At the intersection of the wide crosstown street and the broad artery that cuts up and down through the area, an anguished ballet can be seen. Cars shiver at the stop signal, their drivers grimacing behind tightly rolled-up side windows and locked doors. And into the intersection comes a man propelled by liquid legs, holding a soiled cloth in his hand. His focus is on the windshield, and with disjointed moves he feigns a pass at dusting it. Experienced drivers, with no desire to have the grime on their windshields ground against the glass, drop the windows slightly and offer a coin through the smallest possible slot. It is taken from them quickly, and when the red spot abruptly changes to green cars lurch back into a traffic flow. The dirty-rag bearer, reeling slightly negotiates a ninety-degree turn and begins the float to catch up with his illuminated director and a new line of captured cars.

The area is filled with past and future tenses. For the panhandlers, the "bums" of bitterly romantic depression literature, it is a real setting for the only thing that is anticipated—the night to come and maybe the next day. And for many of the "permanent residents," mostly artists who have for years been moving their materials into loft spaces shielded by the faces of five-to-ten-story light-industry buildings, it is a place to create "the past." A place to be remembered someday as where the pieces and works that brought success were made.

The artists—people who would be artists and people who are artists—are here because there is space and the space can be purchased in monthly quantities at a reasonable

"Nearly ten years ago when I first came here the bums were strictly alcoholic, with nowhere to go. Sometimes they'd ask for money, but some would quote some William Butler Yeats instead of asking for quarters. I gave away a lot of quarters. It was pretty hard to resist them."

—A JAPANESE SCULPTOR

cost. Life in the area is one of little distraction, little subterfuge. And there is accessibility to others who possess similar drives and dreams. A young, soft-spoken film-maker speaks of her loft and her street.

"There's two types of living going on in here and both of them are nearly invisible. One is the business stuff that goes on. Those people stream in at around eight and work at the printing houses and small manufacturing companies that have stayed here, and then they stream out again at around four-thirty. The other is the people that are living here—the work they do in their studios, the wonderful things they are doing.

"When I first moved into this building it was still basically manufacturing. My place used to be the Rolling Eyes Corporation. They used to make little eyes, these pink and blue plastic eyes for toy animals and dolls. Tiny eyeballs. It took me about six months to get rid of them. They were everywhere, in every crack and crevice. And it was weird, all these little eyes watching you.

"I remember when the landlord was first showing the place he was really trying to convince me to move in. The thing he was really proud of, in terms of his lofts, was the curve at the head of the wall. He kept going around saying, 'See this felicitous detail, isn't it wonderful? Felicitous detail.' Anyway, I moved in, and it's worked out well. There are some artists in this building but for the most part they're architects, or film-makers, but I guess that qualifies as 'artist' these days.

"When you just walk through the neighborhood, you know, it's just gray. But once you get to know the place, things take on a warmer color. People aren't gray. Like on

this block. The first thing is the Gulf station. It's an important part of the block because that's where I get my cigarettes. People I know sort of drop in there and they're always telling stories. Across the street there's a trucking garage. I absolutely detest the garage people. I've always had a fantasy of buying it and turning it into a park. The reason I detest it is that when the trucks start going out in the morning the men there all shout back and forth, as though none of them have normal voices. And the racket goes on for two or three hours every morning. But there are some wonderful things too about the garage itself— things that happen visually. Near dusk the trucks come back and as they're parking, the dusty windows over there give off wonderful shadowy effects. The headlights shine through and make patterns— weird, ghostlike shadows. It's nice.

"Just up from the garage there's a tenement house. In that building there's this man who stands on the street all the time and has a little black terrier. The man's in his sixties, I guess. He's white and probably retired. And up on his window facing the street he has this huge sign. Usually it's his roll of honor. Dulles, LBJ, Chiang Kai-shek, and all these weird people. He changes it a couple of times a year. And he has a huge American flag that he carries down the street. Sometimes he wears signs on his chest making some kind of declaration, like on feminism—he was totally anti. Anyway, he sort of parades up and down the street with his little dog—the dog is pretty vicious and barks at everybody—and the man tries to engage everybody in conversation. Whenever I see him I just cross the street.

"There are two other old tenements across the street from him. There are some rather weird people in those, too. There are two transvestites—at least, I think they are. The people in this building keep debating about it. They're absolutely fantastic looking, but they're also hookers. So they come out at eleven o'clock at night in hot pants, high heels, and make-up. They just knock everybody over. And also in their building is what we refer to as 'The Screamer.' I've heard her for two years but I never saw her. Everybody talks about her and fantasizes about why she screams but no one really has anything to say except that she screams a lot. One day I walked out and there was a woman, in her thirties, blonde, good-looking, dressed in normal middle-class fashion. And as I walked past her she shouted, 'Get away from me! Get away from me!' I had seen the screamer! This was The Screamer. She does that to just about everybody."

Men begin lining up on the sidewalk late in the afternoon in front of the Municipal Shelter, a bulky building that years ago was a YMCA. Hot breakfasts and suppers, designed to meet federal Department of Agriculture recommended minimum nutrition standards, are ladled out to those who are present and have twenty-five cents. Across the street, behind a double layer of locked doors, people who are never completely oblivious to the misery that can be brought by the streets work. Many residents of the area, although they could pay the higher rents demanded elsewhere, have found that the scale and perspective of this particular neighborhood can't be duplicated. So they stay and they work. A sculptor who has begun to enjoy the moderate comfort that comes when galleries schedule shows with some regularity has no plans to seek a new environment.

"I came here because it was far away from where I was. Actually it didn't matter where I was to go as long as it was far away. But I do feel uprooted, I am uprooted here and I was uprooted in Japan. And even though I feel a confrontation between the cultures, I can work here and I can see that things are slowly moving—and I have learned that time can't be wasted. It is too late to go back home. I don't mind that it's not pretty here and it is noisy and dirty because I grew up in a city so these things don't bother me. And somehow Tokyo and this place have similar characters—they're busy and they fill the senses. When I came here ten years ago and first experienced the skyscrapers I didn't have to even look up. I could feel them there so it wasn't necessary to just look at them. They're in

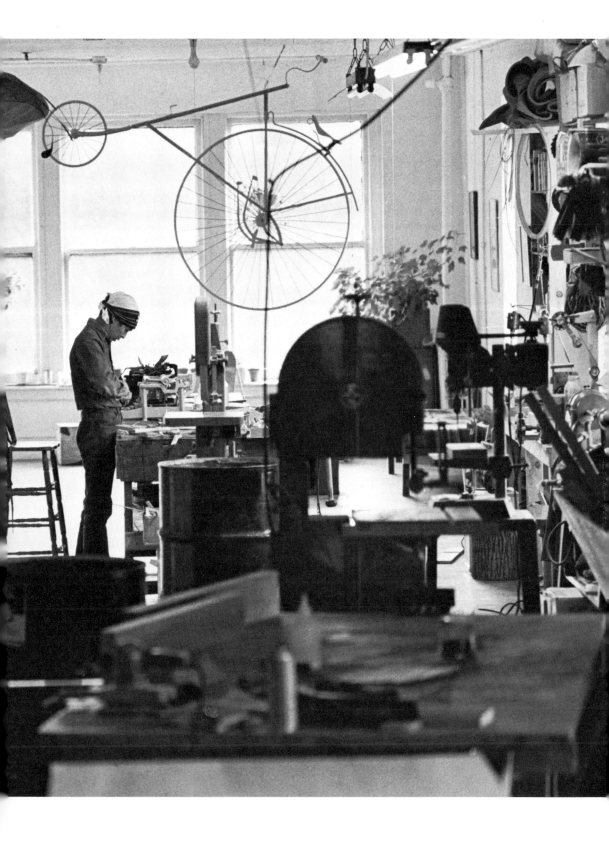

your sense. I think that the only thing that did surprise me when I came here—that I felt and still feel—is that housing is so rigid and strong —all that stone. Coming from a place like Japan, with all the houses made of wood, you feel like you are very sealed in and isolated here—like you are in a grave. I don't think this type of loneliness exists in Japan. It's very isolated here because everybody's living in their coffins. And maybe that's why so many people get crazy and they want to talk to other people if they get a chance."

"Once a friend who had never been in this part of town came down to visit me. He was appalled that on every street corner there was somebody asleep, or screaming, or being bloody, or something. So he told me that there was a guy who was asking for help. We went out, because, you know, I felt that I had to respect my friend's feelings. And we saw this old guy. He asked us to take him to the Shelter just up the street. We helped him into the Shelter and the man at the desk recognized him and thanked us. Then we came out and my friend saw another guy, he was moaning and asking for someone to help. So we helped, we took him into the Shelter. We came out again and walked down the street and at the corner another man had fallen and was shouting and swearing. My friend asked him if he wanted to go to the Shelter. We got him inside and then the man at the desk really got mad at us. He told us to stop collecting people."

"I really think that lots of people on the street don't really belong to the street. Once I was at a wedding reception and I ran into an architect who had his own firm. When I told him where I lived, he said, 'Oh yes, I spend time there.' I thought that maybe he had a studio but he said, 'No, I'm a bum sometimes.' His wife told me that he was an alcoholic and that they were getting divorced because of his habit. It was strange to hear this kind of a story at a wedding party. He was a very respectable guy."

Public People— Private Houses

It has the sounds, the tone, of a small town in the mid-South, a rural town. Under the late-morning sun the occasional creak and clatter of an aimlessly swinging screen door carries up the block. Passing cars kick up clouds of dust from the dirt-caked street. The small houses are structurally sound, at least to the degree that they can sustain rehabilitation. And, because of this, the area is a "target"—an experiment in the use of private funds in a marginal neighborhood that has no status quo. It is either going to be improved as a place for living or its already pronounced decay will accelerate and another boundaried wasteland will be produced. Using a successful neighborhood rehabilitation effort in Pittsburgh as the example, several banks and private foundations joined together, hired a director, assembled a small, young, highly motivated staff, and began to establish a presence in the area. A money pool for home improvement loans was created, and the "office" was given the job of finding people who could not qualify for traditional loans—people who would, if offered them, accept low-interest loans and fix up their homes, in concert with their neighbors. It takes being there, ringing doorbells, getting people together to show how much work the houses need and how the job can be done. It takes time. And, to many of the people living within the "target," time is what seems to be in great supply. A seven-acre pond is only three blocks away, and beyond its reed-clogged waters there are more substantial houses—two-story brick homes of middle-income families. The pond and its grassed shoulders, instead of being a meeting place for the area, serves as a

"The landlord, when he gets what he wants out of this house, then he's bound to say, well, he don't want to renew the lease. And I've paid all his bills and I have to get out and find a lease someplace else."

—A "WELFARE MOTHER"
WITH SEVEN CHILDREN

81

barrier of nearly infinite width, for many of the families in the "target" are "welfare tenants": pivot-points for money sent out by the Welfare Department and passed on to private landlords who live in other sections of the city. For instance, only a few screen doors down from the office—a completely rehabilitated house used by the project staff for their work in showing what the private sector can do in an age of diminishing public money—lives a thirty-one-year-old woman. She has seven children. She has been a "welfare client" all of her adult life. Her youngest child is not yet a year old, her oldest is ten. Her house, typical of many in the area, has a rectangular foundation measuring fourteen feet by twenty-two. There are an enclosed front porch and two rooms, a living room and a kitchen, on the first floor. Upstairs there are two bedrooms. The toilet, sink, and undersized bathtub are on the first floor. The house is privately owned, by a landlord she has never seen. His son, a middle-aged real estate broker, stops by on the first of each month to collect the rent.

Her voice is surprisingly husky. Her smile, when it appears, is sardonic.

"I been in the house for almost a year. Before that I was living uptown. But we got burned out. The building was in bad condition anyway, so we were burned out and Welfare moved us into a hotel. We had to move out of there, you know, cuz of the rent. The rent there that Welfare was paying was a thousand dollars a week. For two rooms and food. I only had five kids then. Anyway, then we moved over to this neighborhood—not this house, but one a coupla blocks away. I found the place and the landlord told me he was gonna fix it up. He never

fixed it up except just enough for me to move in. So I went back to Welfare. They sent somebody out to investigate and they said yes, the place was in bad condition. You know, the kitchen was falling down into the basement, the water was drippin'—our stuff got ruined in the basement. So they told me to take the landlord to court and to pay rent to the court. And after a year running back and forth to the court, the landlord, he told the judge that me and my kids, we tore up his place. It was my word against the landlord. He got the money, the two-thousand-dollar back rent, he got that and I didn't have nowhere to go. I went out and found a new place and I went to Welfare with it. It was beautiful but it was for twenty-five dollars more rent than Welfare'll pay. They told me they couldn't do it, that I'd have to find a cheaper place, and that's how I moved into

the place I'm living in now. I have four rooms and I have to pay two-twenty-five a month to stay here, and all the landlord's expenses, the utilities and all. And there's not enough room, you know, cuz my kids are getting big, especially the ten-year-old. She's starting ladyhood and I can't have them all now in just one place. I have two sets of bunk beds. I put the boys on one side and the girls on the other. But that's too close. The ceiling, when you come in on the porch, is cracked, it's coming down. The landlord, he won't fix the roof except for once when he put a few tiles up over some cracks. But that's not helping. When it snows or when it rains hard again it's gonna come in again. We made an agreement at the beginning that in order for me to get the space I had to pay the electric and the water, but I can't do it no more because I've got a small baby now and the bills are too

high. The last light bill I got was for thirty-four dollars. The landlord told me the water bill would probably be twenty-five dollars for the year. I got a water bill now for one hundred and twenty-six dollars. And I got a shut-off notice for the gas today. I gotta find the gas place so I can pay that money and the water bill's not even in my name—it must be the person who was living here before. The landlord's son was just over here. He came to pick up the rent and I told him, 'No, I'm not givin' you no rent because I'm not supposed to pay your water bill. I'm not buying this house, I'm only renting.' He told me he was gonna give me a dispossess so I said, 'You give me the dispossess cuz I'm not gonna pay your rent and your water bill. Now you gonna have to do one outa the two.' And, you know, when I moved into the house it looked okay. It seemed nice cuz it was clean. The walls was, I guess you'd call it, washed down. I know it wasn't paint. And the living room had wallpaper in it. But then I found out it was leaking everywhere—just like the other place."

One evening a week, behind a boarded-over shop window and a metal-sheathed door, a do-it-yourself maintenance class, organized by the office staff, gets together. The evenings are devoted to wiring—just what is a fuse box, anyway, or how do you build a closet, a storage wall, how do you check roofs and gutters, and just what are basic repairs that you can do yourself? The class is primarily for owners, the resident owners of homes in the neighborhood, for the success or failure of any effort to improve the area is ultimately up to them. The information is about real things, and the tone of the classroom is similar to that of a surgical amphitheater with a group of surgeons in attendance witnessing a new technique. There are a few tenants on hand, sprinkled through the resident homeowners, but nowhere in the room are there any landlords. The "welfare mother" of seven doesn't attend. With seven kids it's difficult to take an evening off.

"There are too many kids, like, in the neighborhood. All of them go to the same school. Like if they have a fight out here on the street they say, well, 'We gonna get you at school!' And they wait for the kids, you know, after they come out of school and they beat them up. My ten-year-old daughter, she's very smart. When she was goin' to this other school she was in a spellin' test with the other little girls. She won. There were fifth-grade kids in the test and she was only in the third grade. Now I get reports that she's not doin' her work right. Because she's scared. I went over to the school and they told me, the principal told me when I asked if I could get my kids bused, that it was too late to do it. All right, but her report card is not good at all and I know she can do it because I've tried her at home, readin' books, and she read every word. So I ask her why she didn't do it in school. The kids pinch her or they stick her, or they doin' something. When you is scared and you have doubt about, you know, somebody gonna beat you up outside, you can't think. And if she gets left back she's gonna be left back not because she don't know the work but because she's scared to death. My kids come home and the bigger kids, they follow 'em down the street and they beat them up, you know, take what they want from them. And it's not only my kids gettin' picked on. It's all the smaller kids in the neighborhood. The bigger ones, twelve, thirteen and up, I guess they think that they're the boss. Other words they say, 'You get smart with me or somethin' and I'll smack you.' When I see it I go out there and I talk to the kids. But if you catch a bigger kid and shake 'em and ask 'Why you doin' this?' they go and get their mothers. And then the mothers get all upset and they wanta fight. And they cursing you out and they callin' you names, you know. A coupla months ago a kid slapped my son and he was crying, saying it was hurting, so I went to this kid's house and I told his mother. I say, 'Your son hit mine here on the face where his nose was cut in a fall.' So she started arguing and cursing. She wanted to fight but I said no, I'm not gonna fight with nobody about no kids because the kids, they're gonna be playing again, sooner or later.

"The city's goin' broke, you know, so they had to cut back on some of the things they had like the tutoring, the movies, and everything, so I guess the kids, they ain't nothing else to do so they just start trouble. My kids, they are home from school at around three-thirty so they just stay around the house. They do little chores, sometimes they sweep out the front, they do their homework, something like that. But it's really worse in the summer. There's no place to go and that's when all the fighting and stuff really gets going."

Traditionally, if an absentee landlord gives up on his property the city, or the state, becomes the owner, the new landlord. There are thousands of buildings and homes on the city lists. They are filled with tenants who find that getting basic maintenance service from the city landlord is as difficult as pinning down a private landlord. And that brings up a question that is discussed frequently in the "office." Why shouldn't the "welfare client" take title to the property? Is there a difference in paying out public money for rent instead of making title payments? Or does it have to be rent so that the people who pay taxes that become welfare monies can be certain that those on welfare aren't getting ahead? Currently, with the political rhetoric about "those welfare gougers," "all those damn people who don't do anything except wait for their handouts," the questions become difficult to address directly. Politicians and would-be politicians can perhaps more easily caress emotions by dealing with straw dogs. They're easy. A mother with seven children (they do not have the same father) has real dogs to deal with. Different realities.

"Man, the dogs, they're getting worse . . . stray dogs, all in the alley, you know, and all over the streets. They don't have no dog-catchers to come around here and pick up the dogs. They used to when I first moved in, but now, I don't know where all these dogs are comin' from, you know. And these dogs are ba-a-ad. They have mange, fleas, they're sick, and the little kids, they don't know no better. A kid that likes dogs will go and touch them maybe, and then go in the house and eat something and

probably get sick. And I don't know, that's not right just because this is a poor neighborhood that you find things like this. Now, in an upper-class neighborhood you never hear of a kid gettin' ringworm or something that you don't know where it's comin' from. Last week a little kid up the street got bit pretty bad. It was by a big dog, a stray, that's been around for three or four days. And somebody called up for the people to pick the dog up but they don't pick it up. Nothin' happens, we just get treated like we is animals, so I guess that's why the kids feel the way they do. The city's gonna be an even bigger mess, that's what I think. People say there's no jobs, that Welfare's cutting back, and like some people are saying that they're going back down South—but they don't go. You can't get no better down there so there really ain't nowhere to go, nowhere to run, so you got to take it day by day, I guess. But I see people getting angrier with each other, and that's what's happening with the kids. The bigger boys, they're the only ones that's got something to do. They go robbing people. Because if you don't got money on the weekend to send your kid to the movie, this kid sits down and thinks, especially a kid fourteen, fifteen years old, he starts thinking and he says, 'Oh, I know what I'm gonna do,' and he goes out there and robs somebody up for money. If there was a place that these kids could go on Saturday and they'd even take 'em to a movie . . . When I was coming up, for instance, like on Saturdays we used to have movies for half price. Everybody get a little change and you go to a movie and when the movie's over, you know, you'd come back and you'd

eat or whatever and then you'd be tired. But these kids don't have this. The parents don't have the money, because if we send our kids to the movie we gotta give them full price. Suppose you got seven or eight kids. Where you gonna get all the money to send them to the movies? Say you get some money together and you send two off to the movies, then the other four or five, they're all mad, they're crying, so it don't make no sense. So the kids go out on the street and they see other kids rob somebody or they want to help them. So it's bad and it's gonna get a lot badder."

Simply because they are there, the people in the "office" have become part of the neighborhood, not working for the city but, instead, making it clear to everyone they come in contact with that they are around because they have jobs. The job is to be around, they have become accepted, or, at the very least, allowed into the life of the area. A welfare mother with seven kids has problems, but the office isn't one of them.

"I was going to school, Welfare was sending me to school. To tell the truth I didn't have much education. My mother, she had nine kids. They sent me back down South when I was school age, but my grandmother couldn't buy me books. So when it come down to reading and writing I'm not good at that at all. And that's why I want my kids to have an education. That way nobody'd be running over them. They'll know for themselves. When the Welfare sent me back to school I was doin' good. But then I got pregnant and I had to get out. It was nice. I was really starting to improve, you

know, and I'm planning to go back to school when my baby gets a little older. I'm gonna try to get off Welfare.

"It's a hard thing when you can't read or write and you got kids. And it's really hard for my ten-year-old. She reads all my mail, she signs papers for me, she puts out money orders for me and everything. And she's got to help all the little ones with their homework because the work they're getting I never had. But that's why I know she can do it in school. And if there's just one thing I want it's for my kids to get 'em educated and I'll do anything I can for that. Everything in their school I go to. If it has anything to do with school, I'm there. Parent-Teacher meetings, and everything else. It can make a difference. The office over there, it's made a difference. The people that used to live there before, I won't go into that, but they used to hang out all over, throwing bottles and all in the street. But after those folks moved

in, that man and his people, at least it began to be clean. People seen him keep his front clean and then everybody else had to do the same, you know, to be comparing. And in the summer he even had the kids out, they would go around sweeping the neighborhood, that was nice, and it looked cleaner. And a while back he even gave my friend a job. When a tree fell in the back he got people together and cleaned all the yards out. That made a whole lot of difference. They're making the neighborhood change some now. Like they've been talking to my landlord. If I could get the landlord to do what I want him to do I wouldn't mind staying here now. Because, at least there's a place I can go to when I'm in trouble, and like a couple of times they let me use the phone, when it was important. And it's somebody to talk to. If I don't know something I can ask. Maybe they can help out or something like that."

Working People

Wine season starts during the first days of October and lasts through Thanksgiving. The Grape Man, who at the end of the wine season will be the Christmas Tree Man, and throughout most of the year is a bus driver, maintains a slightly worried look as in his gravelly voice he directs his young assistants and surveys the grape-filled cartons piled high in stacks on the sidewalk. Early fall air carries the footstep sounds of people walking to the food markets a few blocks away on the avenues. It is a Saturday afternoon and the small espresso bars and social clubs which dot the half-mile-square area are filled with patrons and the counter-melodies that make up Italian conversation.

The wine-grape stand is one of several that have been in the area each fall for nearly seventy years. And, as the immediate environs have changed from a pastoral district to busy city streets, a father and then his son have overseen the business. Similar tenure can be found up and down the streets in small shops—places where dough is kneaded, baked, and sold; sausage ground, stuffed, and aged; pasta turned out from bags of flour and meal; and cheeses shaped by experienced hands. But this is the wine season, and in the cellars of many private houses and well-kept tenement buildings, the day, the weekend, and several that will follow are for working on the wine.

The wine-making is a private affair. It is not a festival or a media event. It is just a personal diversion, subject to the realities of the times. It is a form of continuity, a recognition of a past made up of families and the long journey from the old country. And, to be realistic, it is

"We work for a livin' and we enjoy makin' wine. These people, they don't sell it. They make it but like a doctor when he operates, he admires his cuttin'. It's the same way with Italian people. When they make up their own wine they admire it, they get together, they taste it, they say, 'My wine is better than yours. I make it this way,' . . . you know."

—A SELLER OF WINE GRAPES

a way of making as much wine as one wants to have (two hundred gallons is the legal limit) for the year to come, without ever having to walk into a liquor store. During the same weeks women from many of the older families in the district—wives and mothers and daughters—put up tomatoes, peppers, anchovies, and a myriad of relishes, and for a few days fulfill a rural rather than a usual urban function. The Grape Man has witnessed the slow, inexorable change in wine season activity during recent years.

"My father was right here on this corner startin' in 1906 with the wine grapes. There were quite a few Italian people sellin' wine grapes then. And their tradition, our tradition, has kept up all these years till today. All in all I am, I guess you would call it, the last of the Mohicans. I'm keepin' this tradition, doin' my father's talent. He passed away and I promised him I'd keep his name alive and I'm succeedin'. But today the grape is like the cost of livin'. It's gone, I would say, from two, two and a half dollars a box, up to nine, nine-twenty-five a box. That's for a thirty-six-pound box of grapes. The forty-two-pound boxes are now nine-fifty to nine-seventy-five, which is, I think, very expensive. But I guess it's due to the labor, you know, unions and all that. The grapes, they come from California and it takes them approximately eight to ten days before they arrive here. They come across on freight cars now, containers or whatever you call them. And when they do come in you got to figure what they cost you, what you got to sell them for. And there's a lot of times we lose, we do lose on this because it's very perishable stuff. If you don't sell it within a few days you can make vinegar."

In the cellar the sweet smell of crushed grapes hangs in the air. Pressing the grapes, working the iron-handled crank, is hard work —repetitive, yet purposeful and good-natured. The people themselves are used to hard work, for many of the men are skilled construction workers, skilled laborers, giving their years and muscle to the trades. The times, however, are not good in the trades, for as public money has been drawn back, the heart of the city's construction industry—the building of publicly financed housing—has come to a standstill. A steadily growing number of men in the area have been forced to wait for their working world to resume. The waiting, the crushing long days of hoping that a rumor of new work will be turned into a clanging time clock and the sounds of bulldozers and jackhammers, usually takes place in private club rooms and coffee houses. Cards are shuffled, cut, dealt, and received volubly over small tables, and increasingly strained laughter has become the bitter reality of too many people. The knowledge that grudgingly dispersed unemployment payments and union benefits cannot go on indefinitely gives a chilled look of unstated fear to people who have never feared hard work.

Italian music, not pasteurized "paisan" singing backed up by Las Vegas arrangements but music made and recorded in Italy, blares from the chrome-dotted Panasonic tape deck which lies on a scarred work table next to the whitewashed basement wall. The men take their turns at the press handle, forcing it forward to the music's beat, pulling it back. Barrel staves swell against weathered metal bands with each creak of the handle. It is a good time. For, at least on this Saturday afternoon, the city may be bankrupt but people still laugh and strain their backs and arms and make something that will turn into pleasure in the months to come. Up on the street the Grape Man continues taking orders and arranging deliveries.

"In the old days we used to drop four thousand boxes of the grape on the sidewalk, and that was about three to four carloads every other day. We'd average about thirty to thirty-five carloads a season. Today if I sell six or seven I'm very happy, because, like I said, the grapes, like the times, are hard. And these people that want to make a little wine, well, instead of making three barrels now they make only one barrel, fifty gallons. The reason? Money. The people around here are workin' people, so they just haven't got enough money. People gotta live, they gotta eat, they gotta pay rent or for the mortgage. So they save maybe their quarters and dollars, they scrub along every year so they can make themselves thirty gallons,

maybe fifty gallons of wine. Sure, there's store wine, but you got to remember one thing. Store wine does not got the same proof as the wine they make here. You gotta figure they get eleven to thirteen percent alcohol in the store. When people make it, they make it about twenty percent. Now *that* is a good glass of wine. After you eat your dinner and all, it really makes you digest. And one thing I gotta say here, God bless the old people, the ones that really make this here tradition of ours. We're gonna try and hold it as long as we can. At my age I'm gonna hope that I can continue another ten or fifteen years to serve the public here, to serve them my grapes."

Six small storage rooms open off the main cellar space. Behind their slatted doors individual casks and bottles of wine take it a day at a time, moving through the natural chemical processes which turn grape juice into well-made wine. The small spaces are marked off for families who share their wine-making skills with friends, helping out in order to be helped.

By midafternoon the floor of the main cellar is damp with pulp and juices. And, as the pressing continues, the table is pulled out into the room and covered with trays, bowls, and plates of food brought down by wives and children. The table also has another function, for during the week it is often surrounded by the men for card games or for testing the various wines that have been resting for months in the individual caches. The men, in their middle years, have been members of the community for most of their adult lives. One is a baker, another an insurance agent, one is the landlord, who until recently was a pneumatic

drill operator for a construction company. His landlord status is the result of years of saving from his construction work wages and his wife's pay, and finally taking title to the six-floor building with its twenty apartments. His status as a "former" drill operator is the result of a foreman ordering him to work adjacent to a retaining wall after he had warned the foreman that the location was unsafe. "I didn't want to lose the job so I did what he said," is his only reflection on the moments preceding the collapse of the wall, the crushing of his leg, and the ensuing eleven weeks spent in a hospital bed. Now the building is his business life, and he allots the wine storage areas to the building's tenants. There is no additional fee. The only cost other than the physical effort is for the grapes—a small profit for the Grape man.

"When the wine season's over, and then I'm done with the Christmas trees, I go back full time as a bus driver—because you cannot live on this grape alone. If I had to live on this grape alone, believe me, it can't be done, not on the percentage I make. You know, if somebody makes a couple of hundred dollars a week, then the taxes are taken off, the social security, the city tax, and somebody can't come home with much. And the mayor and the rest of them, if they're gonna keep taxin' us, I hate to say it, but even if I have to travel an hour and a half I'll get out of this city as sure as God is up above, because this is gettin' ridiculous here. But it's a shame. People that made this country, people that come here to America, worked building, concrete, cement, bricklaying, carpentry and everything, they're forgotten—all of them here. And the old people here, been here for forty, fifty years, what can they do? What are they gettin'—a few dollars a month from Social Security? What can they live on, somebody tell me. . .? So who's gonna help these

old senior people? And now it's up to
a younger generation. Those who
are workin' on construction maybe
they got a good job—or the truckin'
business. But if these boys get out, if
they leave, we ain't got nothing.
Because these boys are following the
tradition of our fathers. If they get
out then we're out, you follow?
That's the hope that we have, that
these young fellas will continue the
traditions after my father, after
their own fathers. And if they continue we'll have it yet. If not . . .
there's an end to everything, my
friend, and I hope it don't come
right away."

MOVING ON

We live in an age of urban buzz words and buzz phrases—language symbols which establish a mood but mean little to those who are being symbolized. Decay, Renewal, Ethnic Awareness, Neighborhood Action, Social Restructuring, Minority Reality, Urbanism, Welfare Cheats, Upward Mobility, Fleeing to the Suburbs, Blockbusting—easy sounds to mouth while trying to give definition to shadows, while groping to embrace a status quo. Any large city that had a role in the explosive industrial years of the late nineteenth and early twentieth centuries has a record of individual, family, and group movement. Neighborhoods, the physical areas, become other neighborhoods, and set off seemingly scattershot changes in still other neighborhoods. And the people who lived in an area originally and moved on possess a memory and, more often than not, an awareness of a neighborhood lost. To the new inhabitants, the reality is that of a new neighborhood.

When change occurs in a city it is usually noted and charted in economic terms. Property values. A language that is of little import to people who, by moving out, or in, are driven by a desire to maintain or improve their personal standards. People move. They move because their housing may be deteriorating, or their jobs or lack of jobs dictate relocation, or they feel it's time to take a step up, or they are forced to take a step down. They move. A few at first, and then, depending on how the spaces left behind are filled, others may follow. And suddenly what seems like the "old" neighborhood exists only in minds. Then city planners, political technicians, sociologists, and urban anthropolo-

gists survey, and using economic terms define an area as improving or collapsing. They overlay other graph-makers' indices—color, ethnic make-up, religious preference —and it's time for the buzz words. Walk through any major city and examples can be found every few blocks. And if you stay with it, asking the people who remained or who came into an area where the people who left went, and allow yourself to be passed on and on, the odds are good that you can trace a major cultural migration.

The young minister, a product of the immediate neighborhood, lives in a small apartment next door to the nearly one-hundred-year-old Lutheran church. He returned after seven years spent in seminary training in the Midwest. But the people he knew in his neighborhood, the neighborhood he grew up in, had moved. And although he now lives only two blocks from the home he knew as a child and is a minister in a church he once attended, he did not succeed in coming home.

"My family moved in here twenty-five years ago, into the first project houses in this part of town. We were the first Hispanics, the first non-whites there. The whole area was predominantly Irish and Italian then, there were a lot of small businesses, family businesses, a lot of bars and a lot of churches. This church, its history is German but we were the first Hispanics in it, and my sister was the first baptized here. The changes really began to take place around here in the late fifties. Puerto Rican migration became really noticeable then, and through the early sixties. And at that point the whites just started moving out. They moved up a few dozen blocks over into the Concourse area or even further into the northern sections of the city. It was then that you could see that the buildings were finally beginning to give way. The tenements, they were built originally to house the poor, that was at the turn of the century. They were built for the Irish who were the real poor of those times. And after fifty or sixty years the buildings were finally giving way. And that's when the city really started a public-housing boom. They tore down a lot of tenements and within a ten-block radius of this street four large projects were put up. The projects became black housing. And the Hispanics, they moved into the tenements that weren't ripped down to make room for the projects. Now, when I left for school in the early sixties, sure, the neighborhood was coming down but there still were some family businesses, small stores . . . you know. It was changing from a lower-middle-class area, which it had been when my family first came here, to an upper-poor. But the people here still made up a pretty work-oriented group. Now, when I came back here, seven years later, the total change had occurred. There are almost no whites, maybe twenty to thirty percent are black, and sixty-five to seventy-five percent are Hispanic. And the few whites who are here now are community workers who come in for a short time to work and then move out. There's almost no business and there are not as many bars here as there were when the Irish were here. I don't know what that says, but there aren't that many bars. The housing that the city built here—now it's starting to come apart and the area has turned into one with a great deal of despair and a sense of powerlessness. It's almost as if this area has become a colony of the city. It seems like a forgotten community. When the city budget gets cut we feel it first. The people here were the last to get things and the first to get cut. I guess this is because, you know, you can bypass the area coming into or going out of town by traveling on one of the expressways. The highways bypass us. All you can see from the cars is a haze. The reason I say that we have the status of a forgotten colony

here, forgotten by the motherland, is that there are no politicians around who really speak in our voice. Sure, we have poverty pimps and we have people who talk a good line and they are the same color as the people living here, but they're just playing a game. And living here isn't a game.

"So many people have left. Those that yelled loud, they're gone. Others have just been bought off. That's why, I guess, I think the money crisis could be a blessing, because there's no money left to buy off the leadership. That may be a good thing for the area. But right now what we have is despair. And this is so different from when my family first came here. Then there was a kind of drive—now people have really given up. And in the last couple of years, just the last couple, fifty percent of our student population has been moved out with their families—north and over to the Concourse areas. Their families were burned out. Fifty percent, and that means money. I mean, if you just look at it statistically that means the state money for the schools is going elsewhere. We're in another transition stage.

"This seems to be the second transition period I've been through here. The first, of course, was moving from white to minorities, and from lower-middle-class to poor. And now I see it moving from people to wasteland. When I came back here after the seminary, five years ago, there were still some glimmers of hope. But a few months ago I was just walking through, going up to visit another church, and I stopped to watch a fire. The neighborhood in five years has just totally changed again. And I felt despair and then

anger, because it didn't have to happen. Buildings re-habbed less than four years ago are abandoned. Places are left, you know, just totally fallow, there's no people, nothing. And the few that are left are getting desperate. And for the first time I really sensed it. I really sensed the desperation. And you can see how people can become revolutionaries very easily in this kind of situation. I don't know what the future is, you know, I don't know. But this has always been a community of change. It's always been a transition community, and with each transition the level has gone down. And it's going to change again, it's always in flux, nothing is stable and it hasn't been for a long time. Well, the only thing that seems stable now is poverty, we do have that, and it seems to be staying, and rats.

"I don't feel quite as much desperation in the kids, however, the streets are very effective schoolmasters. And the street teaches you a lot of things very early. So these kids haven't really had a chance to really dream. They've just been going around picking up the crap. They just have no time to sense the future and both the good and the awful possibilities.

"There's another thing here. Most of the residents that have moved in in the last five years are rural blacks and Puerto Ricans from the mountains. They come from family backgrounds, and the shock of this community and this city is so overwhelming that the results are what surround us. It's just so traumatic for them. Nobody's been able to help them make a smooth transition, no one has really helped them. But think about it—it's a frightening thing to come into a community like this after you've been in a family where you know there's some kind of job and you know the church and the school. And they come here and things they counted on become the oppressors. It's a very frightening thing and these are the results. A lot of studies talk about this breakdown in a family situation, but it's not that. It's a special situation in that the parents don't know how to cope. It's not that the parents don't care. I get very resentful when some sociologists talk about that. I think that the city can be a frightening monster.

"I remember when I was in seminary in St. Louis, working with poor white Appalachians. You know they're going to die in the city but their dream was to go home. And they were going home in their minds. And that's a problem, because when you're dreaming to go home, you're not going to build anything permanent. You may die here, but what you're thinking is that you're going home, you know. That's not every minority community in the city but it's here. There are others, like up north where my family moved when they left here—neat little one-family homes, you know, a car, clean streets, the myth of decent schools. It's a mind-set as well as a location. Not too far away there are black communities, upper-middle-class, a lot of West Indians, and over by the bay there are a lot of middle-class Puerto Ricans. I think that the goal of anyone who is still here is to move to those areas, or out. But right here people are caught up in such a desperate state that now we have the fires. Five thousand fires in this area in a year. I think there are var-

ious reasons behind the fires. And I think that there are a lot of things that we don't know, and can't even begin to understand. But I do know that landlords are having some of them set. Insurance companies have collected four million dollars around here and they've paid out nine million dollars. The insurance companies aren't making any money, but somebody is, and there are some parallels and some progressions of the same owners getting most of the damages. There are also junkies setting some of the fires. They burn a building to get copper wire. It's a very dangerous thing but they can get money for the copper, and these guys are desperate. Then you've got people who are still living with the myth that if they get burned out they will get top relocation priority from Welfare. That's a lot of bull, but some people believe that, so some of them pack up and set a fire. And also some of the buildings are so old and messed up that they just go up. But the majority, most of them I think, are caused by landlords and junkies. I had a kid in one of my youth programs who was given three dollars for setting a fire. And it's done shrewdly. One guy comes in and leaves a couple of gallons of gasoline. A couple of hours later another guy comes in and spreads it around. Still later another guy will torch it. And by the time the fire department gets there it's so soaked in that it's a full, raging fire.

You know, the kid that set the fire would never tell me who paid him. Every time we talked about it it was a different person, one time a black, one time a white, the next time a Puerto Rican. All in all he torched three buildings and he said that one time his sneakers almost caught on fire as he ran away.

"I've seen a lot of fires from the street but one night when I was living in the rectory I got to bed early for a change. It was about midnight and I woke up and the room was filled with smoke. The first thing I thought was, 'Oh my God, the rectory's on fire.' I looked out the window and across the street there was a raging fire. Now, I was on the third floor of the rectory so I watched the fire from close to the top of the building, and it was frightening. It was frightening because the people were running around. The firemen were frightened because right at the door was an unsafe building mark. And it was the first time that I had seen the whole drama of a fire. And it wasn't a small fire—I mean, the roofs were burning, and the whole house went and then it started in the neighboring buildings. It was a terrifying experience, but it's symptomatic of the condition of this community. I mean, you walk or drive around the area and it looks like a war zone.

"It's easy to get depressed working here, but things do happen that keep me hanging on. I don't view the church as being different from any other organization here. I mean, if it's not serving the community then it should get the hell out. And I think that when the time comes that I'm not serving the community, and someone tells me that, then it'll be time for me to move on. But until then I try to work and not let the despair get me. But despair does come when you see maybe one kid that you helped and then see two hundred that are going to hell—and I don't mean in the biblical sense, I mean it literally. And despair leads people to two things—either they're going to kill themselves or they're going to throw a bomb. And that's frightening, but that's what despair leads to. Either we take some kind of cop-out, and that's what drugs are, and liquor is, and singing sweet Jesus songs is here in this community. It's a cop-out, it's a panacea. Either we do that or we're going to do the hard work, there's no ifs, ands, or buts. Most of us are doing the former, most of us are hiding behind all these things."

Even in a war zone there are those who linger, who pick their way through rubble and attempt to create a jerry-built immediate world while waiting for earlier days to return. Less than half a dozen blocks from the church, a man and a few friends lounge in their "neighborhood," spending yet another day in observation and conversation. The block resembles a partially completed modern archeological dig, with all but two of the still-standing buildings gutted by fire. Demolition signs will soon replace the soot-marked signatures of the street-level shops and the small stores which were storage shelves for the more than four hundred families who less than two years ago lived here. Then bulldozers and dump trunks will cough into the block, the walls will slide down to a fragmented rest, and the block will silently wait for something to happen. And it's possible that if contemporary mythologists really pay attention, someday they will tell a story about a bird—not a fire-breathing, silver-clawed phoenix, but a barn swallow rising from the ashes and broken stone, and instead of flying off into the heavens it just perched for a while.

"I got a hammer. I got me some wood. I got me some nails. I started with eight beams. My friend, who helped me, he has the hand of art. He knows how to make things. He's straight from Puerto Rico. Him and me put half of the house together. It took us about an hour to make the frame, the balcony, and the kitchen. Then some other friends helped us make the second floor. That took us about three or four hours.

"I used to be the super of a building across the street—the assistant super. It burned and then the next

113

building burned, and the next. The fires, I wish I knew where they came from. I've been around this block for nine or ten years, but I don't know. I swear that to God and I swear to my mother. The landlord, I knew him a long time and I asked him for a place to stay. He said all right, take the other building's second floor. There was nobody there. I stayed there for about three or four months and then, after that another fire broke out. And after that everybody moved out of the block. And I started building my little house.

"The neighborhood, it was beautiful. Italian people, half Puerto Ricans, and colored people. American colored people, you know, and all of a sudden the fires. Whoever set them, he had to be a maniac, at least to me he had to be a maniac. Or it was somebody getting paid for it . . . you know. It got monotonous—the whole block, and it took less than four months for the whole side of the block to burn. The buildings on this side of the street got burned before . . . a year and a half ago. And whoever did the fires don't got no heart because the kids, you know, the kids, and even the grownups just barely had a chance to get out of the buildings. I feel sorry for the number of kids I had to bring down myself. The whole neighborhood, it was my friends. Everybody was my friend here. If I wasn't working and I needed something they would come up to me. Sometimes they used to see me sitting on a stoop with friends, drinking, and they used to come over. They were beautiful people. They used to treat me right. But then, about a year and a half ago, the neighborhood started to change. The whole tragedy started then.

"The people here, half used to live out of Welfare, so they were moved to hotels and apartments. I was the last person who came out of the buildings, and the only way I came out was because five police came in and told me I could not stay there no more. So that's when I started doing my home. I took a chance. I needed a place. I needed four walls, besides, if the fires woulda kept on going in the buildings I woulda got blamed. Because I was the only person still in there. I just decided to do the house. Now four of us are staying here. Two on the ground floor. Two on the second floor. Right now we got a nice group. We do everything together. We share the house and we don't do no harm to nobody. And if we find somebody doing something we'll try to stop it. We don't want no trouble brought in here. I got a sofa upstairs. The water's right at the curb in the hydrant. We wash the dishes there. And I got four dogs— Rusty, Sonya, Negra, and I got another one, a brown one. I had four chickens, two roosters and two hens, but somebody stole them when I was asleep.

"I've never taken any help from the city. I just sit around and people help me out. I don't have to worry about food. If I have to drink, I drink too. For money I ask for quarters. That's what I do. And I'm not ashamed to ask for money, as long as I do no harm to anybody. I ask a person for money—I'm not ashamed because I need it. I need it to eat. I got a mouth. I can talk and people can say no. But I get by."

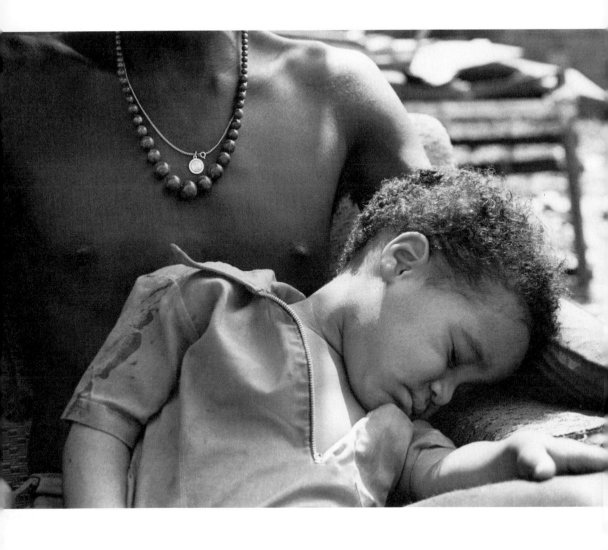

The subway station is two short local stops and nearly a generation away from the old fire-marked neighborhood. A young woman and her husband—they met at college and married at college—can look down from the elevated platform as they wait for the downtown train to take them to work and see the spot at the base of the sycamore tree where her favorite cat was buried very late one night. It is a five-minute walk from the subway to the apartment house, past a small intersection-bounded bench area and down a sloping street.

"My husband and I, we moved in here a year ago. We didn't look too long because we were living in my mother's house and we just had to get out and get our own place. We got this apartment because a friend who lived here recommended us. She told me it was fairly decent. I had told her that I didn't care how big or small our apartment was as long as we got one in an area where I didn't have to worry about being mugged. This seemed like the only fairly decent neighborhood around with a rent we can afford. But in this particular neighborhood it is really the only decent building where you don't have your ceilings caving in on you.

"I never liked this area. I hardly ever rode this subway line before. In fact, I used to hate it because of all the stops. I'd never been around here until my friends told us about the building. They've been living here for three years. They were the first Puerto Rican couple in this building.

"My mother came here from the Philippines. My father was born in Puerto Rico. They got married when he was in the service and came here

after the war when my sister was a year old. I grew up in what used to be called Fort Apache. I was brought up there. First when my parents moved there they lived in the basement of the building. Then, after a few years, they bought the house, so now it's just our family. Three floors and a backyard. I was a tomboy when I was a little girl, always out in the street playing tag and catch with the fellas. We used to play stickball. I was never with the other girls, sitting home playing with dolls. And once I got into high school I never used to go out. Just be in the house. What can you do? Clean the house, sit by the window. That's what I'd usually do. I'd study and then I would just sit by the window and look at everybody doing their thing outside. We didn't have any real recreation centers in the neighborhood. There was a park there, but it wasn't safe even then.

There would always be fights. I remember one time, I'd just started in high school, and I went to the park swimming pool with my girl friend, she's black. We were coming out and some other girls tried to mug us. We didn't have any money or anything. They were just trying to be tough. But there we were, at a very young age, minding our business. After that I just never went back. I was frightened. I wasn't allowed to walk through the park by myself. It just wasn't safe.

"As a kid the only reason nobody bothered me if I walked down the block or up to the avenue with girl friends was because the guys on the block knew who I was. They knew my family, and they knew my brothers. So they wouldn't bother me, simply because I was brought up there all my life. They would never say anything. But when the gangs were around it wasn't safe to even walk up and down our own streets. They'd be fighting and running after one another with guns and you could very easily be hurt. You'd duck when you saw them coming. And at one point in the late sixties it wasn't safe to look out your window or sit on your front stoop without having some wise guys get nasty with you. I musta been in high school, my second or third year of high school. That was when the neighborhood was known as Fort Apache, because gangs were always fighting. And you could see them walking up and down the blocks with chains, machetes, knives and sticks and pipes. And one evening they picked an argument with a family man who lived across the street from our house. He had two girls. He minded his business. He just said something like to cool the

boys off. They didn't like it. So, they came back later in the evening and the leader of the gang, he owned a rifle. But the guy who actually used it was only fourteen or fifteen years old. They didn't like the idea, I guess, that the man had something to say to them. It was pretty late in the evening, around eleven or twelve, and my mother was in the living room with my sister. I was in my bedroom. My mother heard the shot. I didn't hear any of the commotion. I came out after the man had been hit. My mother looked out and there was the kid, aiming from right on the bottom of our steps. He had the rifle and he aimed it at the man, who had probably already forgotten about the argument. Both my mother and my sister were still looking out the window when I came into the room. They didn't know what to do, to call the police or not. They were just hiding because they didn't want to let the kid know that someone saw him. After the kid shot the man, he ran across the street, grabbed up a pipe, and just beat the man to death. The kid was taken in afterwards. He was locked up for a couple of months. Then he was let out because he was a juvenile—a minor—and I don't know how long the owner of the rifle was in jail. He had to do time because the rifle that was used was his. He was an older fellow, in his twenties, and all his gang members were very young teen-agers. They just didn't care. And there was an innocent man who just spoke his piece and got shot for it. Right in front of his home.

"My husband and I, we don't know anyone in the area, just the people we knew at first when we moved in. As far as the people around, if we see them one day I wouldn't recog-

nize them the next day. We just
don't socialize or go out of our way
to see who lives here, you know,
what they're like and what they're
into. We just mind our business.
There are no real recreation parks
around here for the baby. Maybe as
far as I will walk will be the sta-
dium, the park down there. During
the day walking down to the park is
not so bad, but even during the day
things can happen. I do walk right
up the block to shop, there's an A&P
and a Shopwell and they know me as
a customer. But there really isn't too
much here. What's here in stores
isn't really worth time or money. We
just do what we need and whenever
we can get a ride out of the neighborhood, that's when we do a real
shopping. We'll be here, I'd say,
maybe for another year. Our lease is
up then, and after that, if things go
well as far as money's concerned,
we'll just get out and buy a home in
a nicer area. But most likely we'll go
into another apartment building—
but in a nicer area."

In many parts of the city evening courses tend to be built around such subjects as Darkroom Techniques, Transcendental Meditation, How to Stop Smoking, Humanistic Approaches to Living, or Color as an Element in a Symbiotic Environment. But in the middle of a living magnetic field beset by unpredicted flux, self-defense has become a prime subject. And the teaching of self-defense has become a significant profession. The martial arts have been enjoying a vogue throughout the country, but there are certain places where it has an added sense of urgency. The religious and ritualistic elements are less important than the ability to avoid being a victim of mindless violence. The instructor has spent much of his young life learning a city's streets and polishing a determination to succeed, or at least, not be beaten. His small karate studio is in a space that used to house a dancing school—upstairs over a kosher delicatessen. The delicatessen closed a month after the dancing school went into bankruptcy.

"When I hit I want to make sure that I hit effectively. And the only way I'm going to do that is by hard training, hard dedicated training, religiously. That's the only way it can be accomplished. That's why I train my students the way I train them. It's hard work and discipline. There's nothing else. There are no secrets, man, there are no mystiques. Basically the students are just ordinary guys trying to do something with their bodies and with their minds. Most of them are really just trying to find an effective method of defense that they can use for street-type situations. They're just regular high school, regular college kids. Some of them are just in junior high school. And they all want to learn how to fight.

"When I was growing up I never belonged to any gangs or anything. I always kept to myself—I've always been a loner. And I had to really take care of myself on the way up, you know. I've had to hurt a lot of people because if I didn't I would have been hurt. When I was seventeen or eighteen, the first time I thought I knew anything about karate, I thought I could take care of myself in a particular situation. And I got wiped up and down the street by about four people. I thought my karate was together at that time, but it wasn't. I was proud though that it took four guys to do it to me, not just one. But I got hurt pretty badly. Then I said to myself, 'I have to use something more effective than what I have now—it's not working.' So I made it my business to train, to develop myself to the point where I don't experience fatigue. I didn't want to be wiped up and down the damn streets anymore. And I don't want it to happen to my students. I let them know that my school is not meant for kids, man. It's for grownups. And that could be a six-year-old grown-up as well as a ninety-year-old grown-up, you know. It's all in the thinking. I let them know that this is hard knocks, man, all the way, because that's what life is all about—hard knocks. And they get their elbows tore up, their knees skinned, and lumps and bumps and pains—all sorts of things. But out there in the street it's worse. I tell kids' parents the same thing. I tell them that I'm not going to grab somebody by the hand, pat him on the back, and play—you know. Because that would be just wasting

their money. For that sign them up at the YMCA. They get all the patting on the shoulder they want. The dude in the street that's gonna try to take your money is not going to pat you on the back. So I'm hard on them, I'm really hard on them. But they know what they're getting themselves into.

"I would rather teach my people how to fight with their God-given weapons than to teach them how to fire a gun at each other. If presidents would do that, okay, if whoever the hell it is that's running countries would get out there in the middle of a hundred and sixty-first street and kick each other's ass, then we wouldn't lose so many guys. They're the ones that start all the damn wars, and we end up fighting while they sit back on their butts. And they have the nerve to ban us, the people that have to live and survive in the city. They don't give us anything to work with. Not only don't they give us sufficient police, but at the same time they don't let us carry anything to protect ourselves with. So all I'm doing is preparing myself and my students to defend. I mean, I'm not saying we're going to win all the fights, all the battles, but I want to at least be ready, be physically ready, to at least run like hell and never stop if the situation calls for running. The discipline teaches something extra. It teaches the confidence to ignore little things. That's maybe the biggest protection of all. You know, a guy cutting you off when you're driving. The next thing you know there's a big fight. For what reason? Just because a guy cuts you off? So let him cut you off —the hell with him. Ignore it. And the guy that passes by and sticks his

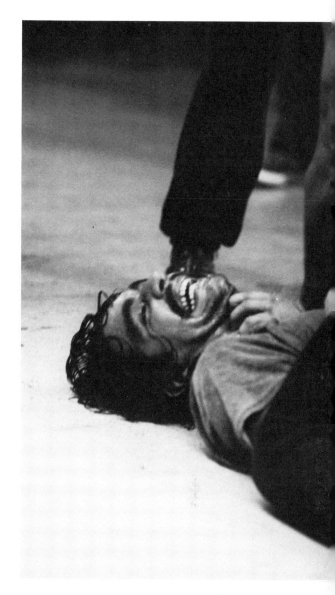

finger, I laugh at that because it has no meaning. I block that out of my mind. And my students learn not to worry about things like that. They discipline themselves to take a certain type of abuse. But if they have to refer to anything, you know, refer to their natural weapons and it's as simple as that. I really think that if everybody had to fight with their bodies rather than shooting at each other, there wouldn't be as many fights. One-to-one there aren't that many people that will get down into a fight. But get a guy a gun, he'll shoot you from a distance any time of the day. BAM, BAM, BAM, but he's hiding. But you call the same guy out into the street and say, 'Let's get down like two men and knock each other's head off,' you don't find many.

"Karate is an art—a religion, actually. It has its rituals, it has its formalities and everything else, but the most important thing on the street is that it can help kids survive instead of destroying themselves. I know what I'm teaching isn't garbage, it's not the Hollywood thing. What I'm doing is taking street technique and camouflaging that with the Hollywood thing. Like, if I get up to teach a technique for breaking out of a hold I can go through a whole ritual about breaking out of that hold. But I don't think they have to go through all that bullshit just to break out of a goddamn hold. You know, punch the guy in the face and it's over. Kick him where it hurts, it's over. Do something practical and efficient because that's what's gonna count. It's not going through an exercise, looking pretty, and all that."

The Concourse stretches eighty blocks from south to north. It was famous and remains famous, and the streets to both the east and west of the tree-lined, safety-isled traffic lanes are part of a complex symbol of former victories and the current losses being taken by a city. It is the spine, the extended central section of nearly a quarter of the whole city. And from its real beginnings in the jazz age it has been more an attitude than an address. A woman who was born, grew up, was educated and married, and gave birth to her children a few blocks off the Concourse —but still very much within the Concourse area—has moved on. But she still considers the Concourse as the touchstone of her city life.

"When I was a child the area, and the areas just below, were basically middle-class white Jewish with just a sprinkling of Italians and a few Irish. But it began to change, and when it changed it became basically Hispanic. Now the bottom two-thirds of the whole Concourse is mostly a Spanish-speaking area. There are a lot of blacks but it is mainly Hispanic. Actually the blacks started to move in first, slowly, in the middle and late fifties. Just a few at first. But it was in the early sixties that things started to turn around and people began to move out. And then, in sixty-five, the state announced the building of thousands of middle-income cooperative houses up near the city line. Then the floodgates broke open. The area still hadn't changed radically at that time. It was happening but it hadn't happened yet. The buildings were already deteriorating and the landlords were letting up on maintenance because their costs were going up. And then the landlords

started to change—the old ones retiring and selling off their buildings. New landlords came in to milk what was left of the buildings. And that's when you could see minority families, welfare families, coming into the buildings. And once you have welfare families, that's it, as far as most other tenants are concerned. So people were looking to move. The co-ops were the answer to a dream of getting away, getting out. Just before the co-ops were announced the attitude changed over from, 'Well, the neighborhood hasn't changed yet, they're not living in my building, we're not having any problems,' to people starting to be afraid. You'd hear about somebody getting mugged in a lobby and people afraid to go out into the street after dark. People were talking about the burglary rate going up and people who had lived in the area the better parts of their lives just became afraid. The schools were the first place that showed real deterioration because there you could see tremendous population changes.

"Anyway, when the state announced the cooperatives at reasonably low costs, then everybody went, 'Wow, this is the answer to a prayer,' because people were looking for a way to get out. I think that in less than a year better than forty percent of my building moved directly into the co-ops. And about an equal number moved out of the area into the suburbs or other parts of the city. I guess that's what happened all through the area. People felt surrounded, besieged, so they just gave up the high ground. They got the hell out. I think that even if it hadn't been for the co-ops most of the change that's happened would still have happened. It just made it happen a little quicker, but the co-ops were not the reason for the change. The reason people moved out was because the change was already occurring."

Usually the young black woman spends most of her day in the courtyard overseeing her young daughter at play. Her family moved into the area when she was a school-girl, just before "the change" began to take place. And, like most people who are now old-timers in the area, the woman is aware of "the change" still taking place.

"This was really an entirely Jewish neighborhood at one time— just a few years ago. And it was a lot prettier. There were buildings with hallways full of mosaic designs and bronze, gold. A lot of sculpture. Now a lot's gone. The building up on the corner of the Concourse, it was really lovely at one time. I've been inside. The living rooms are sunken. All the doorways are arched and very Spanish. It must have looked very pretty once. The floors would still look nice if someone would sand them. And the building's huge. Next to it is a building that people call the Fish House, because of the beautiful designs on the outside. That was really a beautiful building once. Even three years ago. Most of the buildings are kept locked now, so you need a key or someone to buzz you in, in order to see them. It's really changed a lot and gone down. The Jewish families moved, as the cooperatives were being built. I remember that just about everyone that lived in this neighborhood, they all signed up and moved up there. Most of the families that lived in my parents' building, with maybe two or three exceptions, moved up there. My parents, they were just about the first blacks who moved here, that was eleven years ago, and they almost moved away themselves. My father's a musician, he plays the tenor saxophone and during the day

he works for the school board. My mother works for the telephone company, and she's a seamstress in her spare time. My parents are very funny, and I find most Negro people are this way—for some reason they're not crazy about Puerto Rican people. I don't know why that is. I've found so many people that way that it really upsets me.

"I had been away for about five years and when I got divorced a year ago I brought the baby back and moved in with my parents. When I came back the people in the courtyard were mostly new. Before that the buildings were cleaner, brighter. There used to be a more expensive brand of paint on the walls of the buildings themselves.

I'm sorry that I came back, that I had to come back. It's been a year now and I'm still not used to it. It's different. For one thing there's more of the numbers around now. People will stand out in the courtyard and the street all day long and wait for the numbers to come in. Right in the courtyard. They wait, and every now and then somebody comes along and says, 'It was a five,' and people will fall out and say, 'Oh no, I had a two, I had a nine, I had a three.' And they put up some money every few hours. Numbers come in and they play them from morning till evening. It occupies their entire day. I don't know where the money to play comes from, but I know it's not welfare. That's about the only thing that's happening here. Numbers. It's so rampant that I heard that a man is opening a store specifically for numbers, right up the street. Everybody knows that's what he's doing. It used to be just a small shop, and now that's what he's going to do with it. It makes me laugh.

"All in all, though, it's really pretty quiet here. Not that much happens. You don't see shootings and things like that. And most of the people are pretty familiar with each other. For example, in the building that my parents and I live in there are a couple of telephone operators. There's a woman that has two or three children in college. Her husband's a merchant seaman. He travels back and forth to England a lot. But most of the people—a lot of them—in that building have city jobs, like the transit authority, or the post office. There's not much welfare in that building. And there was another woman who lived next door to us—she moved into a rest home two years ago. She was the widow of a man that played with George Gershwin.

"The thing that's strange, you know, about everybody moving is that nobody expected it to happen. My parents, I mean, they didn't come here because they wanted people to leave. They moved here when they did because it was a nice area and they were the most disappointed people in the world when the people they wanted to live with just left. Because then they found out they weren't living where they thought they were."

The "co-ops," an answer to a middle-class prayer offered up mainly by white supplicants, are an urban statisticians' heaven—three hundred acres, fifteen thousand housing units, approximately sixty thousand people, and endless compilations of cubic yards of landfill, tons of grass seed, square yards of sod, miles of tree roots, pounds of cement, lengths of elevator cables, miles of telephone wire, created by a combination of federal, state, and city funds. Figures and statistics are used by the politicians as reminders to potential voters. But the day-to-day measurements that matter directly to people who live in the partially antiseptic, partially parklike setting are simple—the income limits, bottom and top, that gave middle-class recognition and eligibility to a limited number of people, the small down-payment required by the state in order to become a member of the "cooperative," the monthly cost or "maintenance," for the most part deductible from city, state, and federal income taxes; and the school —actually a complex of seven schools, with the most advanced physical structures and curriculum found anywhere in the city.

The legal limits of the real city are only one hundred yards to the north of this "city." And beyond the surveyor's line, true suburbs, with their own pleasures and problems, stretch out as though fleeing from their reason for existence. But on the city side of the line, the flight, at least for a historical moment, has stopped for nearly fifteen thousand families. In the short years since the first families, nearly half of them from the broad Concourse area a few miles to the south, began moving in, the community had developed a dis-

tinct character. It was conceived as a safety valve, a way for a city to hold on to people who could otherwise be expected to leave. And it was accepted by people who didn't want to leave the city but felt compelled to slow the changes attendant on living in a city. It is surrounded, protected from the traditional city streets by two eight-lane federally financed expressways. But regardless of the relative isolation from total urban life, the residents continue to have to navigate the often-changing currents of the times.

A woman, a community worker who moved into the first completed building with her family, and whose parents, the grandparents of her two children, moved into the second building, came to stay.

"The main reason people wanted to move in here was that they were looking to improve their lives, to more or less insure their neighbors. The buildings most of us used to live in were just getting older and when there were vacancies, well, people with any kind of financial means weren't going to move into deteriorating buildings. And that meant that a different type of neighbor began showing up. So then more and more people wanted to move out, you know, because they weren't living with the same kind of people they had been living with. It seems strange now, one of the major reasons most people moved out of their old neighborhoods was because the areas were starting to become black and Puerto Rican. And yet people moved into this community, these buildings, with the full realization that part of it, around twenty percent, was also going to be black and Hispanic. And when I asked people, you know, why—they'd say, 'Well, it's new, this is a new community. This will be a different class of people.' They felt this was the working class, not the welfare class. And now, after a few years here, one of the reasons a few people have moved on again, the reason they gave was that the community became a little more minority-oriented than they expected. At the prices we were paying here at first—the rents and maintenance costs were originally very low—they were willing to be tolerant. But now that the cost of living here has nearly doubled, some

people are no longer willing to extend themselves.

"The people here have gotten a reputation for being pretty outspoken. We've had the rent strikes, fought the state—our note-holder —pretty effectively. And that surprised a lot of people, particularly the politicians. The community was able to show a relatively solid front when something like an unexpected cost increase challenged us. I think that's because people here have a feeling that they are really fighting for their own homes. In a tenement house or even a private apartment house with a landlord there was no feeling of really caring, of really having anything to do with the apartment. You knew that you didn't even own the dust on the bricks. But now people have a stake in their homes and in this community. Making a down payment on the apartments gave us, if not legal ownership, at least the feeling of ownership, a sense that something belongs to us. I think people here do feel that they own the dust on the bricks—at least that much of it. So

145

they have the right to say what they think. Before, living in an apartment house, if there was a problem with the superintendent, or a problem in the building, you called the landlord. Maybe you got him, maybe you didn't, and if you did get him, he probably hung up on you anyway. And people moved here and they found that the management, whether they agreed with them or not, they found people who were willing to sit down and listen to what they had to say. Even if you came in yelling and screaming, it didn't matter. There is someone there— always there. It was just a whole new ball game. So the pressures, the pressures of the rent strikes and trying to determine just who owns what, they're different pressures than what people felt before. Now the pressures at least belong to you. You feel that you have to take a stand.

"The schools, the quality of the schools, matter a lot here. Just about everybody I know with school-age kids felt, before they moved here, that the schools their children were going to were going down fast. The schools were the first place where most people noticed that their neighborhoods were changing. You could walk into the classrooms and notice a change in the type of student, the student wanting to learn or not wanting to learn. A middle-income child, particularly a Jewish child, may not want to learn, but is deathly afraid not to, because if he or she comes home with a report card that doesn't reflect learning something, then they're going to get it good. They can get their heads knocked off. They're not going to be able to get away with it more than

once. Parents are going to sit on them, get them tutors because they aren't as smart as the parent would like to think. But if they're getting bad report cards because they're not behaving or not paying attention or not doing their homework, something of that nature, well, the parents aren't going to stand for it. The parents tend to use the child's work in school as an important part of the family status. That's why the schools in this community are central to the way of life. And the complex is huge, there are nearly ten thousand kids going to the schools in the educational park. They certainly aren't all great students, but the families here are proud just to have children in these schools. That's an achievement in itself."

STAYING PUT

Quiet Neighbor-hood

"It doesn't bother me that
there are cemeteries all over
the place. Of course, this is a
joke, having a cemetery for a
backyard. But we had a great
Halloween party, with the
cemetery out back and all.
Everybody really got a kick
out of it."

—A YOUNG HUSBAND

When the Second World War ended, the area, now twenty-seven rectangular blocks, was a greensward, a no-man's common, filling the space between the borders of four aging cemeteries. Throughout the country the late forties and early fifties were the good times for developers. The boom years. And land previously thought unacceptable for building and selling homes was soon turned by earthmovers. Modern-day town houses replaced the trees that for years had overlooked the headstones, the individual monuments to a city's European heritage. War veterans took VA mortgage loans, moved into the houses with their young families, rented out the extra apartments to families much like themselves, and settled down to suburban life in the city. And although the area is now two generations old and faces have changed, the style has remained much the same.

"I've lived around here most of my life. We got the apartment when we got married two years ago. We got it through a friend of mine whose brother-in-law owns the house. We came up, we looked at the apartment one day, and my wife really liked it so we rented it right away. My aunt has a house near here and one of my cousins lives right down the block. I was familiar with the area, and I know quite a few people who live around here. My brother-in-law lives only about four blocks away. There are a lot of young couples around.

"The area's a pretty good mixture. A lot of Irish, a lot of Jewish, a lot of Germans and Italians. It seems to go by blocks. Down by the church it seems to be more Italian, while the houses right here on the block have

a lot of Germans. Really Germans. And there are quite a few Jewish people around but not right here on the immediate blocks. It seems as though most of the people around here are civil servants. And there are a lot of children—not so many on this block but on the side streets. And, you know, I've never really seen any blacks out here at all, living here. I've seen, maybe, in the two years we've been here, six black people. It's so unusual that you notice. We don't go around looking, but you do notice.

"People are very protective of this neighborhood, of the neighborhood itself. We went away on vacation and I was careful to tell our next-door neighbors that my brother-in-law was coming in to

water the plants—because they're very conscious of everything that goes on. It's not that they're nosy, but they're careful. And maybe they are a little nosy. It's not like a project neighborhood. When you see someone you don't recognize in the area you know he doesn't belong. If a neighbor sees someone ring a doorbell they know that it's not a doorbell to a large apartment building, that it's someone coming to see someone. And if they don't recognize the person they may be, not alarmed, but they do take notice.

"People here seem pretty involved with the neighborhood but they don't seem to be very involved with each other, you know. Like you talk to people when you're hanging wash on the line or if you get involved with things at church. But otherwise people don't really seem to have that much to do with each other. Even people who have been living next door for five years or so. They don't go into each other's houses, they don't have relationships like that. We just talk, you know, on a daily basis about the weather and things. The neighborhood hasn't changed at all since we moved in here. There was a big to-do about six months ago because the gas station right across from the church closed down. There was talk about putting a seven-story apartment house up on the property. Then the church got a whole group together to go down to City Hall to fight it. And after about two months the apartment house was defeated. I think that most of the political activity is a crisis kind of thing. There was some activity over not busing kids into and out of the local schools but we didn't really hear about it. We don't have any school-age chil-dren yet so we won't be involved with schools for a few more years. But I think that parents around here are very active with anything that has to do with the schools. And I know the church is very big on pushing people to be politically knowledgeable, to being active. When it came time to register to vote they held registration in the church itself, to make it more convenient. They encourage activity."

Family Homes

The "restrictive covenant" was broken nearly thirty years ago. In the years since, expansive lawns and flowers and hedges have matured with season after season of trimming. And the oaks which dominate the parklike area of more than three hundred homes have grown taller and their trunks have thickened. It is an excellent testing ground for latent white-liberal racism.

In a city blacks are, of course, seen on the streets—building-lined streets with sidewalks instead of front yards. They are even accepted without an afterthought in luxury apartment buildings in the finest sections of town where rentals to politicians, entertainers, and athletes are welcomed. But on block after block of colonial, late-Victorian, and Tudor homes, most of them set back on carefully tended one-third and half-acre lots? Private homes for private people and private families living private lives at the up-end of the economic scale—people whose names almost never are printed inthe daily newspapers?

It took only a few years after the scrapping of the "covenant" for all but a few white families to make their exit. Most of them moved out of the city, across the tax line, to the official suburbs. But, in sociological terms, the neighborhood changed very little, if at all. Education, real income, family size, automobile ownership, vacations out of the city and out of the country—the standard census yardsticks match closely. The houses, of course, are worth more now, but that's true of any group of well-maintained, expensive homes anywhere in the country.

Changes? It seems to come down to resident pigmentation and an

"When we first moved here this wasn't a black area. In fact we were blockbusters, you could call us that. We got some flack when we came in, the kind which was subtle. Nobody wrote 'Nigger, Nigger, Nigger,' on the tree, or 'Go Home Blacky,' but it was . . . like, you didn't exist."

—A HOMEOWNER

altered sense of history. The other changes are those that occur everywhere in stable neighborhoods as families grow and children, suddenly adults, move on to their own lives and the family homes become the homes of young grandparents.

A woman, a young grandmother, who is, in terms of a comfortable neighborhood if not of the crowded inner-city streets, an activist, is also as close as one can come to an expert on the effort required to keep a neighborhood together.

"Most of the people out here have been here for years and years and years. And like the two of us, they're here to stick, you know, keeping their property even though their children have grown. And when you've been here through most of your life, paid off the house, then what is the point of moving? I realize that I love this house. I'm less enthused about the immediate community than I was years ago, but it's still my community and if I live here I have to be a part of it. So I have to work to maintain it the only way I know. And that's either writing somebody or calling somebody or vocalizing somewhere. That's me, and I don't think I could exist if I couldn't say what I want to say.

"When we moved here—it was in forty-eight—the Welcome Wagon was never put out, let's put it that way. It really didn't make that much difference with us, but I think it may have bothered my mother—she lived with us—because she was always the very, very friendly kind who was used to having neighbors. I couldn't have cared less, at least I told myself that, and I didn't feel threatened. We were the first black family on this block, if that's any distinction, but soon there were more and more.

"We had other things to worry about when we first moved in. We became active in the school because we wanted to make sure that none of the games teachers sometimes play on minority kids were being played on our kids. But there still were games played, you know. The area around here was ninety-eight percent white and all of a sudden the school became fifty percent black. The whites were transferring their kids.

They claimed they were going to live at an aunt's house who had an address in another school district. And within a few years it was only the blacks in the area who were going to the elementary school. And we found that the school began to slip.

"We found from experience in the neighborhood association that people would prize something more if they were paying for it. They could recognize a value then, so two years ago we hired our own private police patrol. We got a terrific response from the neighborhood the first year, and we had a hired patrol on a twelve-hour tour, running from four in the afternoon to four in the morning. We had to charge ten dollars a month, payable every three months. And for a while it was good —very good. And you know, I still think the basic idea was sound. We gave out stickers to be put on windows so the patrol would know what houses were to be checked. But we made a couple of mistakes. We didn't change the color of the stickers every three months, we kept them too long, and it got so that if someone paid thirty dollars for three months and the same orange sticker was being kept up three more months, some people would say, 'Well, the patrol's coming by my house anyway so I don't have to pay this quarter.' And even without the sticker, people felt that everything would be all right because the patrol was stopping by a neighbor's and that was enough. It got so that more and more people began to feel that way, that the patrol was in the community so they were safe anyway. And we began to get a fall-off in response. And now we've come to the end of the line with the patrol because money is tight with a lot of people, it's just not available. So the patrol's ending, after two years, for lack of response. We certainly haven't gotten any better police coverage from the city police, so people are installing more locks, burglar alarms, and more and more people are keeping pretty vicious dogs. And that's what bothers me, I guess, that people seem to be relying on dogs rather than their neighbors.

"It's so difficult, I find, living in the city the way we would like to live. I find it's a fight. If I go out my door in any direction and look I can find things that will make me come home and get on the phone. If I walk down the Boulevard to shop for a quart of milk I can get angry. I walk up there and I see piles of trash next to what used to be a gas station. I get angry because, I think, all of us have put an awful lot of time and money and effort into the property and there's a responsibility to keep things up. I like the good life but I'd also like the community, my neighbors, to feel that this is their community. In spite of what they say about this city we depend on each other for a lot of things, and we're going to have to depend on each other more and more. And I worry that maybe we're losing that. When we send out notices for the civic association and nobody comes —it's a nice night, not sleeting, snowing, raining, or anything, but nobody comes. And you wonder, 'Don't they care?' Do people really have a lack of interest in their own investment? They have a right to demand and expect certain things from their city. And we are not demanding and expecting these things. And it hasn't been just since the economic crunch. So if the garbage isn't picked up on Monday, maybe it'll be picked up on Tuesday. If it's not picked up then, then people begin to call me. And this is what gets me angry. They call me because they know that I'm going to have already called the Sanitation Department. But I wonder, why don't they call themselves? Why aren't people interested enough to call themselves . . .?"

A Rally

"This is what the landlord said to me personally the other day. He said that because a number of people here are welfare recipients, that they don't need any more than what they have—they don't deserve anything better. That was his reply."

—A TENANT ORGANIZER

The streets are lined with trees. And the large red-bricked building, trimmed years ago with white-painted window frames and cast cement detailing, has the look of softly comfortable apartment living. Now the white paint has become the gray that is accepted as city-white, and within the substantial exterior walls there is little feeling of comfort. The building is really four buildings, a quadrangle with three wings facing out to broad sidewalks. The fourth side splits the block and merges with other emotionally unconnected structures. The buildings next door have a different landlord.

The living mood is one of distraction. Concern over whether the lukewarm water pouring lazily from a hot-water spigot will remain tepid long enough to finish washing. There is edginess brought on by the grapevine word that an electrical fire burst forth during the night in a sixth-floor hallway. Will the hall lamps, supported mainly by wires, not plaster, make it through another day and night? There are the continuing parent fears that something might happen again to one of the kids in the unlocked lobbies or the seldom-lit stairways that thread through the complex.

It's almost time for the rally, the first in what some tenants vow will be a series of rallies, continuing until something is done. In a third-floor apartment half a dozen women sit at a dining-room table talking together, joking, laughing, as, using Magic Markers, they transform shirt cardboards into activist placards. This tenant organization is nearly three months old. There were others before, several in the preceding four years, but dissension and disagreement over who should do what and disillusionment when results were hard to see brought them all to unannounced ends. But this time, maybe this time, it's going to work.

"What made me an organizer was what almost happened to my daughter. My husband had recovered from a heart attack and he had just recently gone back to work. He called me and said he was having palpitations and he didn't want to come on the train by himself. So, he asked me to come and pick him up. I was a little reluctant because I don't like to leave the children by themselves. But anyhow, my daughters —the oldest is sixteen—they said they'd be all right. I don't know what made her go outside to dump the garbage because she could have waited until we returned home. Anyway, she did. She opened the door

and the two younger girls, my thirteen and twelve, stood at the door
while she went. At that time we had
cans in the hallway near the stair-
case. She went out, dumped the
garbage, and as she started back to
the apartment this guy came from
the other side of the complex with a
ski mask on his face. He grabbed
her from behind. The younger girls
panicked. They ran back into the
apartment. He threw my daughter
down in the hallway. The younger
girls came back out. One had a mop,
the other had the metal tube from
the carpet sweeper, and they started
to beat the man. About a week
earlier my German shepherd had
died of a heart attack. We'd gone to
the ASPCA and gotten another one
—about six months old. She had just
been nursed over distemper and was
still weak. But when the younger
girls saw that the man wouldn't
turn their sister loose they ran back
into the apartment and untied the
dog. They led her out and as weak
as she was she did attack. She got
the man's arm. He didn't get to
commit a rape.

"My husband and I were coming
into the building when he came out.
The super and a couple of other fellas from the building chased him
into the street, up the avenue. He
jumped into a taxi, rode about six
blocks, and about half an hour later
he attacked another woman right in
front of her husband. We found out
later that he was a psychopath. He'd
been let out from the hospital as an
outpatient and no one followed up to
see that the man was getting his
treatments. He hurt several policemen when he was arrested so he had
to face about a dozen charges. And I
said, 'This is it. It's not close to
home. It is home.' I just couldn't let

this kind of thing go past. Someone
had to really get this building
together. There had been other people trying to organize before but it
hadn't worked. We still had no locks
on the doors to the building. The
halls were dark, and nobody ever
patrolled the halls or the lobby. It
was time to get going. I took two
months off from my job as a nurse
and went to work getting people
together. I just don't feel that we
should have to move into any other
area just to have a decent place to
live. There are a lot of good people
here, the apartments are good-sized,
and we've been paying rent here for
fifteen years. I mean, it doesn't
make sense. All my girl friends,
they're moving out to Long Island,
out of the city, and when they get
out there they have the same problems. So what good is moving and
paying three, four, or five hundred
dollars rent? To have the same problems? I want to clean up this
building. So do most of the people
here. So we're going to make some
noise, wake up the landlord and the
city. And live here."

WOMAN WITH HAND MIKE: This rally is about to begin.
Please gather your posters and
come down and start marching.
You know that television
and newspaper reporters, media,
is here now
on the premises.

We must be willing and able
to fight for your rights.
You are paying tenants
of this complex.
You do not have to be
afraid. Come out now
and fight for the rights
of your building.

We need complete cooperation
of all tenants
within the complex,
that we may fight.

Those
that don't come out
it means that they're happy.
That they don't care.
They're happy
with what they're living with.
They're happy
with the rats.
They're happy
with the roaches.
They're happy
with defective elevators.
They're happy
with a lack of service.
We're tired
of living
with constant fear.

CHORUS: WE WANT ACTION
NOT JUST PROMISES
WE WANT ACTION
NOT JUST PROMISES

POLITICIAN WITH HAND MIKE: It's for the benefit
of our kids.
This is all we're asking.
We're asking the people
who live here
to c'mon down.
To come out.
It's for all.
Please come out and
join the picket line.
Thank you.

CHORUS: WE'LL HAVE ACTION
NOT JUST PROMISES
WE'LL HAVE ACTION
NOT JUST PROMISES

MINISTER WITH HAND MIKE: Ladies
and gentlemen,
we're asking everyone
to come down.
Everyone,
this is for your benefit.
Now is the time
for us to pull together.

There's nothing
to lose by talking.
Everyone,
come down now.
Come downstairs.
Please
c'mon
down.

CHORUS: WE WANT ACTION
NOT JUST PROMISES
WE WANT ACTION
NOT JUST PROMISES
WE WANT . . .

The Community

There are twenty-seven telephones hung on the walls. Men move down the line, phone by phone, dialing long-distance operators. "Yes, Buenos Aires. Person to person collect. I'd like to speak to Mr. Farbringen." They wait for the anticipated answer and then speak again. "He's not in? Then tell him that I'll call back at nine P.M., my time." Calls are placed to Paris, to Lisbon, to Cleveland, Pittsburgh, London—city after city—until each phone has served as the vehicle for the message, the signal. Then the men in the main communications room in the Hassidic Temple relax for a moment. Ninety minutes later, shortly before 9:00 P.M., each phone rings. A small lever at the base of the unit is snapped to the side, and Temples throughout the world are connected with the Rebbe, the world leader of this particular Hassidic Jewish sect. An opening in the wall of the communications room overlooks the main Temple, a high-ceilinged space nearly the size of a football field. By a quarter to nine the Temple is filled with nearly two thousand men, many in place for over an hour. Most of them are bearded, dressed in similar black suits, shirts open at the neck, and black felt hats, and they are assembled out of respect both for the man, the Rebbe, and for the spiritual heritage he represents. The Temple itself extends through what from the street—a broad, tree-flanked boulevard—appear to be four separate buildings. And it is these buildings and a number of others in the immediate area that comprise the spiritual headquarters for over 250,000 people worldwide.

"If there's a meeting ground it's in business, in commerce. Let me do my thing—you do your thing. Don't oppose me —I won't oppose you, and we can get along as neighbors and good friends. It shouldn't be that hard."

—A HASSIDIC JEW EMPLOYED BY THE CITY

171

At exactly three minutes before the hour the Rebbe makes his entrance into the Temple and begins his walk to his chair. His footsteps sound in the absolute silence of his followers as he makes his way through the devoted crowd. Then, seated at the center point of a long, white-linen-covered table illuminated by a series of intricate chandeliers, the Rebbe intones a Hebrew blessing as old as the religious form, and begins to weave his reflections and his vision. Twelve miles above the planet a small silver-metaled globe with the word TELSTAR etched into its thin skin whirls as a way station for his insights and direction. Within the Temple, old, middle-aged, and young men listen intently. Boys, the sons, are also in the crowd, squirming with their youth but remaining conscious of the words spoken to them. And high on a plexiglass-sheathed balcony opposite the Rebbe, women peer down at their men and their leaders. Except for two occasions a year, for the blessing before the High Holy Days and during Shevuoth, when the women meet alone with the Rebbe, the floor of the Temple belongs to the men. The woman's role is primarily that of a traditional Eastern wife—to give sustenance and solace to the men and to care for and oversee the growth of the children. The same aura of dedication is present on the balcony as on the floor of the Temple.

There are twenty-five hundred Hassidic families living in a twenty-four-square-block area spreading out from the Temple. They live as on an island in the middle of a district dominated by black families. There was a time, well into the sixties, when the environs were mainly white, and not only Hassidic Jews, but all shadings of Judaism, Orthodox, Reform, Conservative, could be found. But neighborhoods change. All but the most devoted Hassids began to move: some to Long Island, others, the older families, making the long journey to the comfort of Florida. Still others headed west, across the city and its rivers, to New Jersey. And for a brief time it appeared that the Hassidic community which had originally come into the area in 1940 would also move on. But it didn't happen. A member of the Temple, one of several politically active members of the congregation, gives his impressions.

"The problems began, really, in sixty-six and sixty-seven. People started running, and in sixty-nine the Rebbe announced his decision. He really came out, he took a stand and spoke, saying that running was no solution . . . that there was no end to running. The problem wasn't just here. It was in communities all over the city. But the key to all this, to not running, was in strong leadership, in this case, Hassidic

leadership. The Rebbe is a very strong, a very powerful leader in whom there is trust. And he kept people from taking off. It was difficult, of course, and it is also to the people's credit that they listened. Also, another thing happened during that same period. During the years just before and since the decision to stay, the Hassidic community saw that it had muscle, political muscle, in terms of votes. We used to be looked upon as the Amish of the urban city, but all of a sudden politicians realized that this community was a very powerful voting bloc. Powerful, because our vote is basically cast as one. The trend has been that the vote goes to a conservative type of person, not necessarily the Conservative Party, but a person conservative in image. This means simply a person who won't be liberal, okay? Because basic liberalism and Hassidic beliefs are just too opposite."

In the Temple the Rebbe pauses after twenty minutes of speaking. He holds a small glass of wine aloft to the congregation, and then moves the glass to his lips. At that moment the room is filled with singing as the men burst into a pulsating Russian folk song—the motion-filled, rhythmic folk music of Eastern Europe. Throughout the room men raise small paper cups full of wine, saluting the Rebbe, and his eyes connect momentarily with individual after individual. Then the men drink from their cups and resume singing with the others. Sound rolls through the room as the Rebbe's upper body moves with the steady, rich beat of the music. His eyes rest for an instant on two young boys who are extending cups to him.

"The kids are very involved in the synagogue, it's a very absorbing thing. They aren't ghettoized, really. They go all over. The parents take an active role and the children, they go, they come, they sing and dance, they share with the parents. It's not a situation where the adults have one thing and hold it out for the children when they get bigger. When the children are young they do things, the same things as their parents. And they like to emulate the parents, I think, and by giving them this chance to copy, they love it. They're always looking forward to doing something as a family. The kids, also, though, give an idea of one of the great problems in relation to other communities. In the interplay between most cultures—for instance, with a black-and-white issue—many of the problems are usually resolved by the kids—not the parents—because the parents never seem to get along. But often different kids go to school and somewhere along the line there is a socialization, whether it's in the classroom or in sports, whatever, but they eventually get together. But in this community it's more difficult. Kids go to parochial schools, their own schools—one for boys, one for girls—all the way through the university level. It's like the conservative Catholic education system. And when the kids shop it is in Hassidic stores, they eat kosher food, so there's very little they have in common with other kids. Even the fact that they may live next to other kids doesn't alter it. Basic problems, social issues, exist. And prejudices are pretty deep-rooted. They'll take a lot longer to remove here than in other areas."

The Rebbe nods his head, signaling that the singing shall stop. He is ready to resume. His cup is removed by an elder and once again he speaks. This evening he is telling of the tribulations of his father-in-law during the pogroms in Russia early in the century. The rapt attention of people who share his belief and historical perspective is his. Outside the synagogue, along the quiet streets of three- and four-story town houses accented by small front yards, the security force is on the move.

"Right now there are several two-man cars and a number of footmen. It's a security agency so they're uniformed, they have guns, and each team has a Doberman pinscher. So they're better off than the police. And the civilian patrol is also still being maintained, but now it has a lighter load. The civilian patrol has been out there for five or six years, every night three or four cars with two or three volunteers connected by radio with a dispatcher at the community council. But people felt something tougher was needed. And I'm not talking about just taking a guy off the street and giving him a gun, which isn't allowed, but we hired some people with experience. A lot of the people on patrol, as I understand it, are ex-police officers, men who were laid off somewhere along the line. And there have been some incidents where they've stopped muggings and things like that just recently. And if they see a mugging of a black or someone else other than a Hassidic they get involved just as much. They're for everybody. Everybody benefits. The dogs, though, have made some people uncomfortable. I was at a meeting where a man said that a lot of people feel that it looks like the South again, you know, dogs and uniforms. Some people may take it that way but I don't think they're right. I feel it's not that bad. The dogs are muzzled, they're not all over the place loose. It's not that bad."

Voting
District

"I'd like to get the man in the street to realize that politics is his life—that the education of his children, the health service for his family, the taxes, all of these things are politicial, and he has to get involved."

—A BAPTIST MINISTER

The precinct police station's day-room filled up quickly for the late-afternoon meeting. People entered quietly, arranged themselves as comfortably as possible in the gray-metal folding chairs, and spoke casually with each other while scanning the chalked police business reminders on the green slate information board. "Found, one pair of handcuffs, see desk," "VINNIE'S BACK!" Three young police officers stood near the door trading pressure-free conversation. The people filling the room were representatives of neighborhood block associations and individual apartment house tenant groups. And the meeting was the third get-together aimed at getting a district-wide civilian radio patrol out onto the streets. The precinct station was the meeting place because it would be where the privately purchased base station, a small receiver and transmitter console, would be located. The reverend, the initial force behind this effort at defensively tying together a number of the area's streets of still-stylish row houses and large lower- and lower-middle-income apartment buildings, studied a sheaf of clipboard-attached notes while waiting to open the meeting. He had come into the area and moved his church into a building used for years as a catering hall in the late sixties, when the district was undergoing a change from middle-class Jewish families to—at least at first—middle-class blacks. And within a few months he found himself face to face with the question of whether he could justify his leadership of a five-hundred-member church without getting involved in broader community affairs, in politics.

"I think that one of the first things that came up was the fact that there was just a lack of leadership, a lack of concern. There really didn't appear to be anyone who was addressing themselves to the real human problems of the community. At election time people would come around to the church and ask for our support, and when the election was over, once they had won, that was the end of it. I think that's why I opened the neighborhood office, it just seemed that there had to be an office where people who had problems—housing problems, welfare, social security, whatever—they could know where to come when they had a problem. And that's basically how I got involved. It didn't seem that anybody else was doing it. It wasn't because I had any expertise—I have no expertise. But I did know that if I could be there when people needed something, that whatever expertise I did not have, I could pick up the telephone and call someone, call an elected official or a city agency. I could write a letter. And because those people seem nervous when they hear from a minister or a church, they'd get answers together. That's how I got started."

The reverend took his practiced stance behind the rostrum and opened the meeting. His round-toned preacher's voice, requiring no electronic help, filled the room. The day's agenda included a summary of the work that had been done in the preceding weeks and an invitation to other groups to join in until, ideally, every street in the large, disarmingly attractive area was represented in an effort to reduce the edginess that was growing in the minds of people throughout the district. Later in the meeting the first checks, representing actual shared payments from the various groups, would be turned over for the purchase of the precinct-based equipment, and specifications and prices

for equipment for the block patrols would be studied. Then it would be up to the individual representatives to report to their groups and select the hand equipment to be used in reporting actual violence or untoward movements on the streets. It was the fourth meeting of the day for the reverend, and although it was not yet time for supper he had been shuttling back and forth between his community office and his church for a dozen hours.

"Physically I think this is one of the most beautiful, one of the most attractive, neighborhoods in the city. But that's part of our tragedy. There is so much to offer and the area has so much potential and yet there just aren't enough people trying to develop it, trying to maintain the stability that the people of this community should have. And it's one of the few integrated areas in the city. One of the reasons I've become involved in trying to get the black community to work together with the others is not because I'm so hopped up on integration—that's not my problem at all—or that I'm so hopped up on brotherhood, whatever that word means. But I just feel that if people can't get together and make things happen here, than it's not gonna work any place. Because the problems here are common problems, not just being experienced by one color. We should have a common goal and that's finding a way to preserve this community."

Half an hour into the meeting the reverend gave the rostrum over to a police officer, a precinct community affairs specialist. He introduced himself and explained that the captain had requested that he take a few minutes and explain to those in attendance—there were now over fifty

people in the room—a new, five-million-dollar program. The program, funded by a combination of federal and state crime-prevention monies, was aimed at providing radio equipment for civilian radio patrols. And although the end result was similar to the program that the people in the room had been working on for months, there was a difference. The government program would result in a minimum of ninety percent of the cost of street equipment being covered by the grant; there was only one stipulation, that all the equipment to be used throughout the city had to be purchased from a single specified equipment dealer. And there was something else, that since the program was in its start-up phrase, it would be six months before the money would be available. Then things could start. As he read from the thick program booklet, people in

the room seemed to settle back in their chairs and pay less than full attention. A woman, the representative of a large apartment house, shook her head and muttered softly to the man sitting to her right, "Don't need it. No way it's worth it to lose half a year and save money we already raised." The reverend sat near the door and listened intently.

"Part of the tragedy for the area is that we've been portrayed, especially as regards the black community, as being a kind of elite, sophisticated community. Maybe there are more professional black people living in the overall area than in most parts of the city, but it doesn't help. Because we make up perhaps one of the most retarded political communities in the city. We elect people but then they just sort of disappear. We get very little service, very little concern. And our voter turnout, it's low. Maybe it's because people have been turned off by politics, I don't know. But I do think there are so many people who just feel that politics has nothing to do with them, that it belongs to somebody else. And one thing that at least some people around here want to see done is to get the man in the street to recognize that politics is his life. But the degree of political nonsophistication here is really unbelievable. Registration is low, and the actual number of people who come out to vote is even lower—particularly in primary voting. And the primary here, that's it, that's the key thing, because this is basically one-party politics here and whoever wins the primary wins the election. I mean, ten to fourteen percent of the people in the district who are eligible to vote come out and vote in a primary. The party has around twenty-one thousand people registered, and in the last assembly primary where the man was elected, there were only twenty-seven hundred votes cast. And there are one hundred and twenty thousand people in the assembly district. And that's why politicians court a white vote here. I mean, in the area the Jewish population is only, maybe, ten or twelve thousand, but they vote, they can determine the outcome of any election."

When the police officer completed his extended statement, the reverend returned to the rostrum. A man sitting in the front row shook his head and said loudly, "Isn't the city broke? I've been told there wasn't any more money, even for jobs." The meeting continued for another twenty minutes, a follow-up meeting was scheduled, and the consensus of the people in attendance was that the official program might save a few dollars, not that many dollars,

and nobody had asked for it anyway. The necessary money had already been raised from small private donations. As they filed from the room the people handed their deposit checks for the base station unit to the acting recording secretary. Hopefully, within no more than six weeks, a broad-based civilian patrol would be on the streets.

The reverend walked the several blocks from the precinct station house to his community office, in the warm late-fall twilight. The streets, with fragments of crushed glass and refuse scraps randomly scattered in the gutters, gave a slightly shabby look to the fronts of well-scaled, single-family stone houses.

"There is no rallying point. In fact I think people are getting even more turned off. That's it—I find that trouble will either crush or it will make

jobs, who are the victims—and the irony is that they're also the ones that have the solution in their own hands. If people would just get together and vote they could get something started. I just maintain that a big part of the answer is massive voter registration, massive voter turnout, because somewhere along the line poor folks and people who are hurting, who live here, have to let people know that they are here. By getting rid of the people who can but who don't deliver.

"It's difficult to get someone to listen. They listen, yes, but I don't think they listen with their hearts —that they listen enough to get involved. And it just seems that this whole political thing, this whole governmental thing, is a kind of private enterprise that is in the hands of a few people. And I don't even blame the people with power, because people who wouldn't be part of the system permitted it to happen. And the average man in the street, he says, 'Oh no, I can't get involved— there are other people handling that,' not realizing that he's the guy who has to do it.

"Still, with all of the city's problems, with all of its heartaches, its contradictions and conflicts, I can't imagine being anywhere else. And there are others, others who stay, complain, fight, struggle, and try to make an area and a city what it can be. It's funny, in spite of the fact that someone can walk around right now and get mugged, or my house might be getting broken into while I'm sitting someplace, it's still worth saving. It's worth it."

people stand up. And I think that what's happening in parts of the city like this, maybe all over the city, is that disaster and trouble— the economic troubles—are tending to crush people rather than making them stand up and fight. But I think that trouble could, it should, make people stronger, more determined. But I don't see it right now. But there's gotta be some way out of these times. And I keep goin' back to that old thing about the polls. It's the poor people, the people who don't have jobs, or who are losing

On the Beach

The small community of weather-beaten bungalows nestles on the bay side of the peninsula, seeming to ignore the open ocean only a few hundred yards away. It feels like a summer place, and since early in this century it has been a place for getting away from the city without leaving the city. When the bridge that arches across the ecologically questionable ocean backwater went up after the Second World War, a few old-timers winterized their small houses and stayed put after Labor Day. And then in the turbulent years of the early sixties more summer people, now nearly half of the hundred and seventy families who own bungalows, began to make it a year-round home, a refuge from a city that was becoming unfamiliar. But it remains, at least socially, a summer community, with a distinct season that starts on Memorial Day, reaches ripeness by the Fourth of July, and ends, abruptly, the morning after Labor Day. During the long, sun-filled, sand-blown days between the beginning and end of the season, the beaches are busy with sunbathers, and the social clubs, with their well-stocked bars, are busy night after night, filled with men home from their middle-income city jobs on the other side of the bridge.

The last weeks of the season are aimed directly at the big weekend, Mardi Gras, a festival of games and costumes for the kids and bigger games and slightly more exotic costumes for the grown-ups. And some beer, some whiskey, and maybe some more beer. Mardi Gras is an end-of-summer party that has become laden with tradition and filled with the kind of memories that can only grow where people have de-

"Three of my four children have bungalows on the beach. We're permanent here and my oldest son's gonna be a permanent. My mother's down the beach, my brother's down the beach—that's how it grows. That's one thing down here, don't say nothing about nobody unless you know everybody on the beach—because everybody's related."

—A PERMANENT RESIDENT

cided in advance that they are going to have a good time. The parades—there are two, a children's parade on the first day of the three-day weekend, and the adults' on the second—are the central events. And like epic media events such as the Super Bowl half-time extravaganza, the costumes and the floats, small enough to be borne on Red-Flyer wagons rather than flatbed trucks, mirror the attitudes of the revelers.

The community, a private cooperative with its own security force, volunteer fire department, softball league, and churches, grew from a cluster of summer tents propped up on the sand just before the outbreak of the First World War. And it has grown as an extended family. By the mid-fifties the bungalows had filled the fenced-in area, and a few years ago, when the federal government

took title to all of the undeveloped land within sight of the peninsula's point, the limits to growth were fixed. Today, when an opening does occur, when a bungalow is put up for sale—and that is rarely—relatives of current residents get the first opportunity to buy. It has been years since a relative didn't buy almost immediately.

Long summer evenings, with long-drawn-out nightcaps at the clubhouse bars, and the chilled and quiet winter nights give time for reflection and conversation and for forging strong opinions about this small part of a city and the rest of the city across the water, stating feelings and arguing them.

"I drove a cab for fifteen years and I'll tell you when the city started to go to pot, and probably the whole country. It was when the civil liberties started coming up. With Kennedy and then Johnson, they took it too far. And they told everybody that you got to like everybody else. That's when the city started going on a downgrade. That's when crime and everything else became rampant in the city. When I used to hack I used to work sometimes in the black areas and I thought nothing of it. And I'm not saying that the civil rights is the direct cause of all the trouble, there are a lot of other contributing causes also. But that's when it all started. Then when Martin Luther King got killed you started having your so-called race riots—they were never really race riots because they were all confined right to the black communities themselves. But it was a kind of a general say, aw, hell with the world. And it's not only here in the city, it's probably the whole world. I don't know. I do know that when I

was a kid, if I was hangin' out on the corner and a cop came along and told me to get off the corner, I got off the corner. I'd say that crime in the city has a lot to do with the financial problems, also, like in the schools."

"In my experience in driving a cab you can't take a kid today who's brought up in the streets and make something of him. You know, you take these kids growing up in some of those areas and you put them into a school. Now in school they're all to themselves, so to speak, and all they got to look up to is the druggie, the guy that's on a corner pushin' the drugs. And the drugs, that's another reason we have so much crime in the city. And what happens? A policeman I know, he stopped a guy uptown. There was a state inspection sticker on the car but it had

out-of-state plates, so he stopped him. The guy tried to get into the glove compartment but he wouldn't let him make the move. He had a loaded .32 revolver in that glove compartment. And there were a hundred and fifty decks of heroin in the trunk. So my friend arrests him, goes to court, and the judge lets him go on a thousand dollars bail. That is not terrific.

"The thing is, I don't care whether it's black, white, whatever, the thing is crime is runnin' rampant. And this in turn costs the taxpayer money. You gotta pay for the cop, he's doin' his job. He goes out and makes an arrest, brings a guy into court and the court has no choice because they don't have enough room in the jails, so they just let them back out on the street again. And all the while it's costing us money. It's costing money for the

jurors, it's costing money for the judge—I don't know where it's gonna end.

"Things can turn around. Things swing back and forth and in my opinion for a lot of years it's been swingin' over to the left. And I pray to God that when it does start to swing now it doesn't go all the way to the right. If it starts to swing to the right too much then we're gonna be in trouble again. And I don't want a police state either.

"One thing down here now, thank God it's a community where everybody knows everybody. But even down here you got a few kids here that, well, they're wisenheimers, you know. But that's gonna be, no matter where you go or what you do. And even if somebody doesn't like somebody else there's a certain amount of respect for everybody. And I think that goes for most of the kids too. And that helps to make this a nice place to live.

"I came from an Irish neighborhood, it was pretty good. On the west side of the avenue it was Irish. Then on the other side it was an Italian neighborhood. Just a few blocks away there was a German neighborhood, and you had an area which up until a couple of years ago was almost strictly Polish. Now you have one side of the avenue that's black and the other side is Jewish. There are still some beautiful streets out there, I mean, you ride down them and you'll see signs still that say, "This is our block, yours and mine, please keep it clean." This community right here is a neighborhood but from my observations, in my opinion, the city has been getting away from neighborhoods. Before, when all these ethnic groups settled in, they had neighborhoods. They were people that clung together. And then when things started to spread apart there were just no more neighborhoods. Like I

had a friend when I was in the navy. He was born here in the city. Now, he couldn't speak a word of English until he went into school. All he could speak was Polish. He went to the butcher, he was Polish. He went to the candy store, they were Polish. He went to the bar to get a bucket of beer for his father, they were Polish. And he walked down the street and everybody knew everybody. And even where I grew up, maybe I didn't know everybody but I knew most of the people in the neighborhood. That to me was a neighborhood, a place where people knew each other, even if it was only by face. Even if I didn't know somebody's name and they didn't know mine, you still recognized each other.

"Today you got people living in an apartment house and it could be a beautiful neighborhood, a co-op or an apartment house could be a neighborhood, but unfortunately people are too busy in their own little worlds and they don't always have time for each other so they don't become neighborhoods—just a house that houses various people. And you can be livin' next door to somebody for fifteen years and you may not even know what they look like. Maybe you work days and they work nights. And that's why I like being here. Because, here, this is a neighborhood. This is a place where people know each other, they're interested in each other. A while ago we had one family on the beach that was in a little financial trouble, you know, rough straits, illness and everything. We ran a dance for them down at the church. And we had a fella down here who had a automobile accident on the bridge on New Year's Day night and was crippled. The people here pitched right in. No qualms, no ifs, ands, buts, or anything. We had a party for this kid and raised a couple of thousand bucks to set up a fund. There's still a fund. It was turned over to his mother. Ironically this same man, he's in a wheelchair today, his father died suddenly late in the summer. And the people on the beach decided right away to go around, they went around and made a bungalow-to-bungalow collection. And, you know, it's kind of nice to live in a place and know that if something happens to you, well, the people here, they're not gonna let you go. Nobody lets anybody go. Everybody belongs to everybody."

PLANNERS

City-towns, semifull service communities within full-service cities, have been built with increasing frequency since the pre-nostalgia days of the Second World War. But nothing really started then. Plans for large, self-contained, inward-oriented communities were being detailed and scaled decades earlier. The sudden difference after the war was that instead of constructing enclosed housing for unskilled and semiskilled workers, new communities were needed for people in the middle of the nation's economic scale. And it's possible, probable, that the creation of large insular cities within cities is what life will be increasingly like in the years to come.

There were "projects" when low-cost, government-financed public housing was stressed in the New Deal years. Then came garden-apartment complexes and planned communities. And more recently, condominium communities, cooperative villages, total environments for living. All are places where people identify with the physical reality of their living complex as much as with the other people living there. The complexes are similar, at least in scale and singularity, to the "cities of tomorrow" that were the delight of world fairs early in the century. And when a lecturing social scientist announces that what now seems to be happening is a "reverse ghettoization" and pauses for reactions from his audience, nothing really new or startling has been stated. It's been happening for a long time now.

There have been modifications, changes. There are "marketing considerations." Give the community its own enclosed schools. Lay out as few internal streets as possible, add a self-administered security force and sports facilities—not only playgrounds for the young but athletic complexes for the parents of the young. In complexes that are middle-income and above, whether "fear" is the selling agent, or education, or health, selling is required, for it has been quite a while since there was a valid lack of middle-class housing. And those were the days when the first middle-class "towns" were erected on the wreckage of neighborhoods that, by mid-century, had deteriorated.

The buildings were laid out on a grid, with seven playgrounds and a large open green and a fountain in the center. A woman who was only a few weeks away from being a grandmother when the complex was first opened has watched its transformation from a raw construction site to an area of apartments and lawns and sturdy trees. During the nearly half of her life that has been lived here, she has seen a granddaughter be born and grow and move on to her own life.

"We're pretty ordinary people here. The group that I know best are more or less intellectual, but the others, they're all right, too. It's not an exciting place, really, as far as social contacts, but I'm so impressed, so overjoyed, I get a real lift just looking out of the window and seeing the trees, the changing of the seasons, as though I'm a farmer's wife. And there's a bird, a blackbird, he makes an awfully nasty sound but he comes back every year. I've gotten to know him and I hear his raucous call. I don't know if he has a mate or just why he comes back. But I can stand and look out there, look at it and feel good.

"My granddaughter, when she was about seven or eight years old, she wrote a little poem which was up on the bulletin board on Parents' Day. It went, 'Out of my window I can see / The bright red berries of the hawthorn tree. / All around the lawns are green. / Thank you, dear old town, for what can be seen / When I look down.' Now that really epitomizes this kid, but of course I had to drag her over to the window and make her write it. She didn't like to write, but that's what came out, that's it, and that much is worth a whole lot.

"This place was built nearly thirty years ago—it was when they were tearing down slums and, as a matter of fact, this was a slum area. I happened to have been in the City Council then, so I was close to it. I got an apartment here for myself and I got an apartment for my daughter. She had been living in a small apartment when her husband was in the army. And shortly after he came home she was pregnant and they needed an apartment. Well, this was brand new and it looked bare, but it was gorgeous. It looked like paradise. The streets hadn't been paved yet when they moved in. And the trees were just little saplings, not much shade. But I think it looked beautiful to everybody who came here. When it went up, the rents seemed fantastically low, and it was chiefly for the boys who were coming home from the service. They were all coming back and there wasn't enough housing because during the war everything had stopped. There were no materials and there was no labor. But then, as the war ended, this place was built. The people here haven't changed much. It was and still is a mix of working class, policemen and people like that, and professionals, lawyers and others. And you naturally gravitate toward the kind of people you're

comfortable with. But there aren't any real distinctions here. There are never any real fights that I know of, even among the kids. One playground, though, used to be the Catholic one. Another up near the fountain was I think where the Jewish boys had their games. You know, there were things like that. But now the children mix much more.

"I'm a city person. I was born here and grew up here, so I guess I'm always aware of what's going on. And I refuse to be a prisoner of an apartment or a small area. It's a very personal thing, and there are people who are inclined to be hysterical, but I'm always looking around —everything fascinates me so. I talk to people, a lot of people I probably shouldn't talk to, all kinds of funny people. Just the other day I was walking down to the library and I got into a conversation with a Puerto Rican man. He said something to me like I was a beautiful lady. I don't know exactly what he said, but things like that happen all the time. I don't look on everybody as being a mugger—maybe that's it. They're not, but I also try to be careful, and I am careful, but funny things do happen. I was on a bus. I was going to meet my granddaughter for lunch. I had to get out at a certain place and I tried to tell the bus driver. The man seated next to me said, 'Where do you want to go?' I told him and he said, 'I will push you off.' He was a Hungarian, a big, burly workingman in working clothes, and we got talking. We got into this whole conversation about Budapest. Now the reason we got into this conversation was that I said, 'You shouldn't say you'll push me off, you'll just tell me where to

get off, no, don't push me off.' It must have sounded funny if anybody was listening. I enjoy it. "Sometimes I do get involved in things that are really silly. There's a store just a block down from this complex. It's a secondhand store, on the corner of that block. I always pass by there, it's a terrible-looking place, it looks like a den of iniquity, and I always look in. It's black in there, crowded, no lights, dirty. And there is always furniture standing out on the sidewalk. Anyway, one day I dared myself. I said, 'I'm gonna go in there and look at it.' I had no intention of buying. And I went in and I saw what looked to me like a player piano. We used to have a player piano at home when I was a kid. And a young woman came over to me—there were two young women there and they were messy and dirty-looking. The woman asked me what I wanted and I said, 'Is this a player piano?' And she said no. I was standing right by the door because that's as far as I would go in, I wasn't going to walk into that room. But it looked—frankly, when I looked at these two young women I felt I could handle them. As I was leaving I asked the woman if they bought furniture. I feel overcrowded in my apartment. I feel I have too much furniture. She said yes, and I said, 'I have a sofa.' I thought I'd get rid of one of my sofas, and then she asked me if I had anything else. And I thought and I told her I had an old clock—two old clocks. She asked for my name and phone number, which I gave her, and then walking home I was angry with myself for doing it. Anyway, I came home and tried to call my daughter, she wasn't home. I wanted to tell her what had happened. And I also

wanted to ask my next-door neighbor to ring my bell to check and see if I was all right. But nobody came that evening. The next morning, though, the bell rings and here is this young man. He looked very nice, he might have been my grandson. He was a Jewish kid, he had an awfully funny name and he was a tall, very good-looking young man. He said he understood that I had a couple of old clocks. Well, I stood him off because I wouldn't sell the clocks until I talked to my kids, they might want them for sentimental value. I wasn't going to let them go easily. The young man was flashing money around and I tried to tell him that I wasn't destitute. I said, 'I don't want to sell the clocks, I have to ask my daughter and find out whether she wants them.' I also have a watch, my father's Omega, which I got out of the closet to show him. And he talked and talked. We forgot about the sofa—he was just arguing with me about the clocks. And he said why couldn't I call my daughter right then. But I said no, I wasn't going to call her at the office, no, I don't call her on personal matters at the office. When he first walked in the door he offered me fifty dollars for the largest clock. But by the time he was here and talking he upped it to sixty-five. He really wanted the clock, but I said, no, he couldn't have it then. So, as he was finally leaving he saw my dining table, a big, solid oak round table. It's really too big for this apartment and he looks at it and says, 'Oh, I'll give you fifty dollars for the table.' He didn't even really study it, he just picked up the cloth and glanced at it. I don't know, maybe I was tired, I don't know—I sold him the table. He gave me fifty

dollars, unscrewed the top and just lugged the pieces out the door. I went back into the apartment, looked around, and said to myself, 'I have no table. That man took my table.'

"I went back to the store again the next morning. He just looked at me blankly, and I said, 'Well, you know I have no table,' and he broke up. I said, 'It's very funny but I have no table.' He said, 'You want your table back?' I said yes, and I thought, gee, this is really a sweet guy, he's gonna let me have my table back and I'll know a nice secondhand furniture guy. He told me to come by the next day. So I did. It was a Saturday, it was pouring, but I went back. And when I got there he said, 'I sold your table.' I looked at him and I said, 'You sold the table already, imagine!' So I'm without a table. I have to go shopping for a table."

Because of the location, close to the business center of the city, individual interests and concentration tend to be directed toward the larger city—an active relationship with the city. A university professor who moved in with his wife when he was on the instructor level and through the years has assisted in raising three children can, free of the distractions that come with transient living, spend time considering problems circumscribed by more than the immediate neighborhood limits.

"I sense security here, not a neighborhood. It may be a physical thing, part of the original planning, and I don't know whether it was clever or just an omission, but there is not a single community room in this entire project. The only community activity, the only place where there is any give-and-take conversation with other than close friends, is in the garage area and in the laundry rooms. And also, I think, around the playgrounds for those who sit on the benches. But otherwise there is no real contact. If someone wants to have a meeting and fight something, take a stand on something, the meeting has to be held off the premises. I feel that's a deficiency. A neighborhood needs a place for an assembly. If there were a place here maybe some people would have got-

ten together, but I don't think it's that kind of a place. There is no real cultural identity here, it's more economic, and I think that real cultural identity has been destroyed throughout most cities. It was destroyed by various expressways and the blind ways administrations went about putting up housing projects, destroying, relocating vast neighborhood sections. For instance, when this place was built, it first had to be decided that some of the slums that filled the streets that were here had to be destroyed. There were many people living in those buildings and they had to move out. And for years and years there were large open spaces throughout this part of town, several neighborhoods were destroyed, and the land was empty until these houses were built. And after that, as all over the city the pace of construction accelerated, more and more neighborhoods were destroyed. And no one paid much attention to relocation, although there were certain standards to follow. The people that were moved out were never brought back in. And the only common bond in many of the new housing developments has been either poverty or affluence. But no cultural ties, no traditional feelings of neighborhood. And it's ironic that now politicians talk of ethnicity, or 'ethnics.' I think that the emphasis, instead of being a cultural one, has become political, and the people are being viewed not in terms of what they can offer culturally to the overall community but how many votes can be cast, how many elections can these votes insure. At least the people living here don't vote just because of their addresses. I think it's a pretty enlightened community and they tend to address issues, rather than be addressed themselves as an issue."

The newspaper advertisements promised the best of the city and the country. Village living without forfeiting any of the cultural and industrial advantages of living in a huge city. And the rolling countryside that surrounds the California-style, multistory attached houses is indeed within the city. The surrounding area is an effective challenge to "myths" about city crowding and the urban inability to feel the rhythm of the seasons. It is a community that was built without relocating anybody or anything other than the natural inhabitants of a large meadow. And young, credit-strong families accepted the offer to have their children attend suburban-type schools and enjoy the safety that is usually purchased only by flight. Conceived on the other side of the nation, it was to be a new, planned town, a series of "villages" which would total nearly five thousand people and approximately twelve hundred homes. But plans change. Economic factors intervene, and instead of a community with its own primary schools and its own extensive shopping facilities, it's a complex of three "cul-de-sacs," or, in more prosaic terms, three small rectangles, each opening to a perimeter road. It is a community slightly less than half the size of the original conception. Five hundred and sixty homes, approximately two thousand people, and no school or shopping center. But the way of life purchased with the homes that were built is considered just fine by most who came in search of the city-country.

An active resident, an attorney who gave up on the legal suburbs and, in an effort to get in slightly closer touch with his career city, came to the city-country, found what he was seeking.

"I don't know when they actually started this project, but when they did start selling the biggest problem was that they couldn't deliver the houses as fast as they sold them. We moved in about a year after it was opened. And a few weeks later I was asked to go to a meeting because someone knew that I was a lawyer. After I had been there for about an hour I went to the bathroom and, strange as it sounds, when I came out they told me that I had just been elected chairman of the residents' association. And I've been active in the community ever since. The main thing that we do in the residents' association is operate the common grounds. They're owned jointly by all the residents, and we're responsible for overseeing the swimming pools, the tennis courts, volleyball and basketball courts, the playgrounds, and the walkways. Everyone who owns a home here is a member of the association, there's no other way to become a member, and everyone also pays monthly maintenance charges for the grounds. It's up to the committee to collect and it is a considerable amount of money. But it's for a pretty ambitious program—keeping a staff at the pool, running various programs. For instance, we channel funds to a youth committee for a football team, a swimming and a basketball team. And now we've expanded the bylaws and we're going to spend our own money to get the streets repaired and put some pres-

sure on the city to improve bus service—that kind of thing.

"We came here because we didn't want to move into a staid, more established area where there might be only one or two children on a particular block for our children to play with. Here they're just crawling out of the woodwork.

"Nothing is black or white, there are advantages and disadvantages to everything, but on balance we're happy. We love the house, we have plenty of space here, and we're comfortable. And we've found that, by and large, our neighbors are wonderful. I'm not saying we get along with all of them but we've made many, many friends here. There's a warm spot based in part on the fact that when a child gets his report card in school not only are you interested but half a dozen of the neighbors are also. The school, the elementary school, is about three miles down the road, and it could be the finest in the city, but it's getting rap-

idly overcrowded. It was built back in the eighteen-nineties, and before these houses were built there were maybe seventy students in it. Now there are around three hundred and fifty, and the facilities are antiquated, but we're not going to see a new school soon. But the faculty, it's first rate. Also, if somebody's sick in the family there will be three or four people over to ask if they can run errands or anything. So it's really tightly knit in the sense that people go out of their way to be nice to each other and to do things for each other. And the common grounds are fantastic. They draw people together because during the summer everybody is out there, at the pool, on the tennis courts. So you make stronger friendships because we're not just seeing people in their homes but a little more relaxed on the grounds. There are parties during the summers, dances, that sort of thing.

"Now that we've been here for a few years I still think it's one of the nicest places in the city, and it has a different atmosphere than the rest of the city. It just feels safer, and it's not that we haven't had any vandalism or crimes. But people will play cards until one or two in the morning and walk home, walk through the common grounds and feel quite safe.

"There is architectural control here. No one's supposed to do anything to the exterior of a home without the approval of the architectural control committee. It was set up to protect everybody's investment, and, of course, it's a very sensitive subject. If a guy across the street wants to put up a gazebo or a pink storm door, whatever it is, to him whatever he is doing is in the finest taste. His. Even if he puts a rubber frog on his lawn he likes it and it looks nice to him. But it may offend some people who have different taste. But anybody who does something thinks they are doing it right. And one of these days something's going to happen and we'll have to go into court and set a precedent. The association's ready to do it, but it gets pretty touchy.

"We've had some problems—particularly for our teenage population. They were uprooted from other parts of the city. They've got marvelous facilities here during the day in the summer, but at night and during the winter, when the commons facilities really aren't usable, these kids have nowhere to go. There's no corner candy store for them to hang out at, there's no community center, there's no public school within walking distance that would be open in the evenings. So we've had the kids hanging out on the common grounds and out of boredom, frustration, we've had some vandalism, some problems. The association took a strong stand. We were concerned not only about the vandalism, but that someday, sooner or later, if the problem isn't stopped we're going to find a kid who has fallen into the pool one night while horsing around and somebody's going to walk in there one morning and we're going to have a serious injury or a death on our hands. Anyway, we decided that if we caught anybody breaking in we were going to prosecute. Because of our complaints the local precinct staked out the swimming-pool complex. And one night they caught six of our kids breaking in. I don't think they were vandalizing anything but they shouldn't have been there. They were playing

cards, it was a rainy night, and the police arrested them. The precinct called me and told me to appear in court the next morning. But when I found out the kids were being booked on a felony for burglary, instead of a misdemeanor for trespassing, I went down to the station with my wife. We spent all night there with the parents and the kids and finally convinced the officers to drop the original charges down to a misdemeanor instead of a felony, so they could be released and go home. The association board met on it. These were our own kids and we had to decide what to do. I don't know if it would have been the same had they been outsiders, but the upshot was that we decided we didn't want to give our own kids criminal records. The incident has been very well publicized and we felt that a lesson had been learned. If we hadn't thought that a lesson had been learned we probably would have gone ahead and prosecuted. These were all teen-agers so we put them under the supervision of one of the directors of the board, repairing all the prior pool vandalism—painting, plastering, doing what had to be done. I called the district attorney's office and said, 'Our kids are still going to school with these kids and we see their parents at the supermarket and at the pool, and I think the lesson has been learned.' The district attorney was most gracious and said that because we had our own rehabilitative program, that if we wanted to come in and dismiss the charges without ever getting into court we could do that. And we went down there and did it. I don't think it's going to happen again."

It is surrounded by a moat, actually a major river, and connected to the rest of the world by a standard moat crossing, a bridge, and a nonstandard crossing, an aerial tramway. It was conceived and designed as another of those experiments in modern living, with walkways, parks, a recreation center, and housing for every income range. And schools— advanced experimental schools —real neighborhood schools that could be reached by students without crossing a single traffic artery. The state announced the Island with the fanfare befitting the turning of a futuristic fantasy into reality. But as the first families, middle- and upper-middle-income tenants, began moving onto the Island, plans were already being revised. Funding, bonds, interest rates, things that cities are built of, are problems that cannot be put off even by the dreams of urban planners.

At the end of the first year participation in the new island way of life was a reality for only one hundred and fifty or so families. And the massive quadrangles which were built to house "senior citizens" and another one for "moderate-income" families were completed but unoccupied. Rumor-filled conversation had it that the state wouldn't open them until the more expensive buildings on the west shore of the island, the buildings with heroic skyline views, were occupied by high-rent-paying tenants. But two thousand housing units were completed, and soon—it couldn't be put off forever—even the lower-income buildings with overviews of the huge generating plant opposite the eastern shore would be lived in.

The setting is idyllic, insulated from the transient life of the central city; yet, in theory at least, it is only minutes away from the action and glamor. But during the early days it sat as a place for romantics with an income—people who could afford to be "city pioneers." And for a woman who had returned after a couple of years of being "out West," and away from city life, it filled the desire for a place apart and a life just a little different. It was one more city adventure worth undertaking.

"I still had out-of-state plates on my car. And as I made the turn onto the bridge I was hesitating, you know. And this truck driver behind me was impatient and he screamed at me. His voice, it was sarcastic, said, 'Hey, lady, go back where you came from!' And, God, he made my day. Because there, right across the river, was the hospital I had been born in. So I really was back where I came from, by God. And more to the point, back where I wanted to be.

"I came across that bridge, and like I say, the truck driver just put me in the right mood. And I looked at this Island as a place to live. I don't think the buildings on the Island are particularly attractive. And yet there was just a kind of ambience about the place as I drove around following the signs. Then I walked into the model apartments and I thought they were charming. The rooms seemed well built and they're all lovely. Whatever the hell the rent was going to be, I was ready to pay it. I had already looked at a few other places, but I knew that no matter what the hell the rent was I would be scrubbing floors, moonlighting, if I had to, to pay the rent. So I pay the rent. The people here

are interesting, just a wide assortment. And of course the fact that we're the first perhaps has something to do with it. It's kind of fun being a sociological experiment. Like we were discussing the other night whether or not we should have a bumper sticker identifying us as residents here. And I kind of agree with the chap who said that there's going to be resentment, because there's talk about trying to keep people off the Island. And that's something to consider, also. Why should people be kept off the Island any more than they're kept off any street or avenue or any other city property? I think all it will do is develop a resentment. And I think that once the newness, the uniqueness, of this place wears off people won't bother coming across the river anyway. But I think that if you try to stop anybody coming then it's going to be a problem.

"We're all aware of little differences. We all know that one area is going to be low-rent housing. We all know that another section is to be seniors. We know that this area is condominiums and the high-income group. And I wonder if that might not cast a pall on the initial experimental kind of thing. It's true that everyone will be congregating in the local community center, in the shops, and things like that. But I'm not sure that that's enough. The initial experiment with the Island, the original idea, as I understand it, was that all socioeconomic levels could live together. I don't know. Here they've color-coded the buildings and it would probably be quite all right if perhaps it was simply to identify your address and not your economic status. If it's going to revolve around the thought that, 'Oh, that's the Jones boy who lives in the Orange Building,' I don't know. My idea had been that as long as they are going to investigate our income, and of course there is that, it's a little bit of the big brother aspect. But I suppose that's a fact of life. But as long as the idea is that people here are working people—there will not be welfare people on the Island—and if everybody is working and pulling their weight, the idea should then be that they should have an equal opportunity for attractive home settings, and it should all be wide open. Like first come, first served. Of course people may not resent the color coding at all. I don't know. Hell, I know I'm not about to resent those people living in the condominiums. I mean, I am conditioned to realizing that we are each of us dealt a certain hand and we have to play the cards as they lay. Now I think I've done the best I could possibly do with the hand I was dealt. And so I might be envious of other people, but I don't think I'll be jealous. I think there's a difference between envy and jealousy. And I really don't know when the state is going to occupy those lower-income buildings. Target dates have a way of being postponed on everything. Everything has been postponed month by month, so I don't really know. But I don't care right now. I'm having a ball the way it is. I really am enjoying it."

LIVING THERE

Walking through a city, riding its noisy, crowded transportation, living in it, is to experience a barrage. Witnessing the heroic honesty of some of the people who live as parts of a city and experiencing the purposeful misinformation put forth as scenario elements by the people who run things, both politically and economically, leaves one slightly limp and feeling the way I imagine an atomic particle feels after being bombarded in a nuclear reactor. It is the barrage, I believe, that marks the only real difference between contemporary urban living and the mentally edited attitudes of simpler places and times. But there is also a steadiness, a solidness gained by stopping occasionally and being reminded again and again of the incredible insight and emotional power that comes to virtually everyone as a result of surviving for a while.

When I began this book I had for years been impressed by the city and carried an anguished pride at living in a city. But I learned many things during the months of being able to move throughout a city as a observer-participant. One, the words "city" and "neighborhood" as things to be praised or cursed are merely distractions. Politicians can attempt to gain emotional power and erratic votes by taking a stand against "cities" and for "neighborhoods," but it doesn't really mean much. What does mean a great deal, and what I find myself in awe of, are people, not plain people for I don't believe in that label either, but the kind of people you don't see self-consciously stating something in 120 seconds or less for a television crew which itself is always anxious to move on to the next entry on their assignment sheet. For instance, several months ago I sat on a stoop talking with a man whose life has been spent in the midst of one of the "rapidly decaying" areas of a city.

At the time I discounted some of what he had to say about his perceptions and life within his personal neighborhood. But in the days since, much of what he had to say has come back. He said, among other things, "I have a very large suspicion that keeps gnawing away that there really is a plot going on. I mean, this is an ideal neighborhood for executive types, just fifteen minutes by train from downtown. The only problem is that you have to get rid of the blight, and by blight I mean us, the people that are in this neighborhood. And so if we get burned out completely and the land lies fallow for ten years or so, then somebody's got a gold mine, they really do. You can build up some nice housing, a lot of the houses here can be re-habbed. But first of all you've got to get rid of us all. There's no hard information but that's what I see as possibly happening." At the time and at that place the word "plot" had an extreme ring, but a headline in a paper a few weeks later made the words come alive. CITY'S HOUSING ADMINISTRATOR PROPOSES "PLANNED SHRINKAGE" OF SOME SLUMS. And the article that followed the headline sounded as an echo of the street conversation.

"A planned shrinkage approach would not involve pushing people around," the administrator explained, but might include such steps as no longer spending housing rehabilitation monies in those slum areas that are already characterized by large stretches of

225

abandoned and razed buildings and a "very marked" decline in population. A planned shrinkage approach would also include "inducements" for people still living in the areas involved to move to other neighborhoods where there is a "continued willingness to live" despite problems. Meanwhile the depopulated areas involved would remain vacant "until new land uses present themselves. . . . I'm not trying to discuss something inhumane. I'm not trying to discuss forced migration," he said. "Don't make me sound like an ogre—I'm not pushing people around."

The least surprised people in a city are of course those directly involved. They know what is happening all the time. And that's another thing that I've seen during these months. Nothing happens suddenly in an urban environment. Acts and directions are announced with stunning suddenness, but the actual setting up and allowing of things to "take care of themselves" extends over months and years. There are very few surprises for participants. Surprises are a luxury to be experienced or enjoyed by spectators.

It is probable that the future of the city, any city—not whether there will be cities but what they will be like—is already at hand. It's in the insights and voices of people who live there. Some of the voices have scared me, others have left me with sadness, but like a chorus the sound is of nerve and hope. And if for a change—and it would be a change —the people who have the job of politics would listen, really listen, and represent the strength and knowledge of the people who happen to live in a city, the future might work. People. That's all any of us can ever be. And that's not bad.